MW01048529

Night Vision

NIGHT VISION

The Powers of Darkness

ROBERT GRAHAM

With illustrations by

MARIA BURNS

MATRIX

MATRIX

Published in Great Britain in 2000 by Matrix
An imprint of Dilston Press, Hilmarton, Calne, SN11 8RZ, England

Dilston Press Limited Reg. No. 3411422

A CIP catalogue record for this book is available
from the British Library

ISBN 0 9536631 2 4

Book designed and typeset by Andrew Burrell

Printed and bound in Great Britain by
MPG Books, Bodmin, Cornwall

www.Matrix4Books.com

THIS BOOK IS DEDICATED

TO

Jane Roberts Butts

MAY 8, 1929 – SEPTEMBER 5, 1984

One thing I have learned in a long life: that all our science measured against reality is primitive and childlike . . .
Albert Einstein

We are what we think. All that we are arises with our thoughts. With our thoughts we make the world.
The Buddha

. . . basically, consciousness has nothing to do with size. If that were the case, it would take more than a world-sized globe to contain the consciousness of simply one cell.
The Seth Material

You are a Gestalt of electrical actions. Within the physical matter of your chromosomes there are electrically-coded systems. These are not the chromosomes themselves. The chromosomes are the physical materialization of the inner electrical data.
The Seth Material

When they are seen as fields of energy, human beings appear to be like fibers of light, like white cobwebs, very fine threads that circulate from the head to the toes. Thus to the eye of the seer, a man looks like an egg of circulating fibers. And his arms and legs are like luminous bristles, bursting out in all directions.
From A Separate Reality, *Carlos Castaneda*

Contents

List of Illustrations

NIGHT VISION

Preface

Twenty years ago, I was handed a book by an Australian, Dale Pike, whose father owned the Spanish hotel, a converted olive-mill, where I was living. I had bumped into Dale and his exotic girl-friend, Jasmin, several years before in a clothes shop on London's fashionable Kings Road and we had become friends. The book had been left behind in one of the hotel rooms that looked out onto the Mediterranean sea beyond the fields of evenly-spaced olive trees. Dale had by then read it from cover to cover and was now insistent that I should do the same. I had better things to do I politely explained in my growing frustration at his repeated attempts to foist on me this dubiously-titled text that pretended to be written, rather absurdly, by an Egyptian deity.

Whatever next! I finally agreed to read a few pages and to offer him the inevitable verdict that exactly as I had predicted, its content was indeed the most absolute of nonsense. A few nights later, I had gone to bed as usual and decided to read just enough pages to convince Dale of my compliance to his wish that I join him in comprehension of the esoteric and world-shattering significance of this dog-eared book that I was squinting at in the half-light of my candlelit room. I began to read slowly and without conviction, through the first chapter of the still off-puttingly titled, *Seth Speaks*. As my eyes grew weary and my mind drowsy after the day's exertion on the tennis court, I drifted into sleep with the book lying open at the page reached, upon my chest.

Up until that day, the hour of that night, I had had no conception whatsoever of the existence, let alone the imminent possibility, of psychic experience. Like most others, I would rather have believed in the flatness of Earth than the likely intrusion of any otherworldly and alien phenomenon into my routine and very mundane life. But on that night, some contact from long ago had by the mere process of my addressing once more this modern version of ancient knowledge been re-established. I woke fully within the dream. I experienced from within the dream state, standing there on the gravel of a familiar English courtyard in the dream version of my physical body, the sudden contraction of that astral body which was initiated by the surging of energy from the base of my spine, up the spinal column and into my head. I knew nothing then, as I panicked and woke in my Spanish bed, of those seven spheres of invisible energy named chakras, that had seemed to contract one up into the other, up my spine, in preparation for my flight, as a sphere of comet-like electricity, streaking across the black night in the direction I vaguely calculated in my stunned silence at breakfast, of Spain.

Nor, as I mumbled a few words of explanation to a concerned Dale – 'I just went whoosh' – did I realise that, as I later read when finishing the book on my return to London, there were indeed triggers in some way inserted within the rhythm of words which would according to the Egyptian author, prompt such a sudden immersion into alternate reality, and the consequent provision of subjective evidence and proof as to the veracity of his ancient message. All these years later, I have thought it useful to set down on paper in book-form what I have discovered in the intervening

PREFACE

period in case it will be of value as a bridging text, a synthesizing of information that may strike the casual reader as being at least as ludicrous as I once believed, until he or she is tapped upon the shoulder by the invisible hand of an unseen messenger.

At the least, it is hoped that this short book, composed of brief notes hurriedly made in the distant and recent past and as rapidly transferred to form a continuous and with luck, coherent text, will reveal with science and esoteric knowledge not yet known to science, how the evolving and co-operative consciousness of genes may be triggered into new and constructive patterns of behaviour through the inwardly focused mind's influence over and control of their pre-physical mental prototypes that are directly encountered through the mobility of consciousness and insight of the man or woman who has ventured into the abyss of the unknown. It is also hoped that this revolutionary book will change the way you think about Life, your life and the life of your body . . . .

ROBERT GRAHAM
January 2000

XIII

Prologue

It has been the grand pretence of modern science that existence is fully comprehensible to the human mind. The great majority of scientists choose still to believe in this comforting myth. That is their right or genetic predisposition. Whether we choose to blame Queen Christina of Sweden for the advent of this secular faith, for permitting René Descartes too brief a time to read from her library of esoteric texts before receiving his philosophy lessons at five in the morning or congratulate Descartes for the metaphysical error that has led to the death of European grandeur, to the invention of the guillotine and the technology of the industrial revolution, the fact remains that the age of enlightenment that he might have initiated in his discussion of the pineal gland, failed then to materialize. Instead, scientists continue to delight in his definition of the non-human species of planetary wildlife as being the unfeeling machines existing therefore solely for the laboratory experiment, and not for the divine purpose of their own evolutionary fulfilment.

Over three hundred years later, our science has so confused as the result, the material universe with being its own source, that only the enlightened scientist who is in the minority, realises what Descartes had deliberately, in his exoteric writing, overlooked: that there is a built-in evolutionary mechanism within the subtle energy levels of the human body, that connects to the pineal gland in the brain, which may be stimulated into a widening of perception to include the pre-physical and immaterial layers of existence. The development of this latent, psychic vision and power to materialize directly without the intermediate science of technology, is of course predicted for the New Age and to be triggered by the effect of seventh ray energy on the spinal column.

The difference between the scientist who believes only in the existence of matter, and the enlightened scientist who does not, has been compared to the contrasting behaviour of the actor who realises that there is an audience beyond the physical stage upon which he performs his rôle, and the hypothetical actor who does not. Or to the difference between the woman who has woken fully within her dreams, and another who has not. The beady eye and the yapping tongue of the televised scientist who pretends to a near-complete understanding of Nature, belong not to the world stage but to the kindergarten; such is the level of her ignorance about the matter of consciousness, about which she knows next to nothing. Yet there has never been an experimental result from any of science's laboratories that, when interpreted in the cool hour and by the enlightened mind, does not repeat the proof of consciousness' existence within all matter, which is the appearance that consciousness takes to experience the physical universe. In other universes, consciousness may appear within entirely different camouflage which is itself conscious and evolving.

The truth about the origins of Life is not often told: that the entire universe, down to the genes of our bodies, emerges from a timeless source, from which it pulses into existence, in each instant, before becoming momentarily reabsorbed within this more primary medium that may, however, be accessed through the intermediate environment of our dreams, into which the woman who has achieved a degree of enlightenment may step in full consciousness. She thereby becomes involved with the creation and direction of events, including bodily events which will subsequently be experienced physically, and in this process, merges her outer consciousness with the source consciousness of the inner self or soul. And by relieving to some degree the inner self of its rôle of generating events for the physical self then to experience in line with those beliefs, desires, and expectations held by the physical self, we emerge from evolution as the conscious and compassionate co-creators of our lives and destiny.

There are, then, two sorts of scientist: one which can see and the other which is blinded and unfortunately still in the majority and to be found on those governmental committees which seem to require as the sole qualification for membership, the persistent belief not that there is an orderly and planned progression in Nature but that She is the creation of chance chemical reaction, producing the genetic structures which we are therefore justified in changing. Though these political scientists would each readily accept that consequences remain unpredictable and global catastrophe may in the future result from their tampering with genetic systems and the additional cruelties being proposed in the name of outdated and Darwinian nonsense, they believe as well in the continuing docility of electorates during the extended period of experimentation. How shocked they would be if this also turns out not to be the case; if the reckless scientist and his political or corporate paymaster were later to be subjected to summary justice in the name of the general will. And how ironic that the very processes of thought responsible for this idiocy remain beyond the understanding of science's most eminent thinkers. We have the absurd situation of being advised by science as to the safety of food products already fouled by science, when through the other ear we listen to the new generation of physicist for whom the fundamental and non-local nature of the gene is pure mystery.

NIGHT VISION

The enlightened physicist operates not from blind intellect but from its blend with intuition, with which she wakens of a sudden or gradually through the widening compass of academic speculation, a member of this invisible audience from whose company and insight she will increasingly benefit, until such a gulf in comprehension has developed that she hardly can associate her previous colleagues with this ancient and new science of consciousness that is being revealed. She feels that by her contact with these overseers of Nature's co-operative evolution, she is being returned to the magical truths of the kindergarten where memories of an otherworldly past still linger in a child's thoughts, and glimpses of the supernatural still intrude upon the imagery of her mind. To this physicist, to her rapidly developing etheric and clairvoyant vision, the human body is no longer seen as the machine of so many genes, but the form taken by the condensing light of consciousness. She perceives directly the existence of an interlocking system of consciousness, which includes that of matter, mind and spirit.

The relationship between the physical glands of the human body, in particular the pineal gland, and their underlying, prephysical counterparts in the etheric and dream versions of the earthbound body, are explored in this text from both the esoteric and scientific viewpoints. From this synthesizing of two traditionally opposing fields of knowledge, we are shown how the transmission of thought and imagery through the resulting multidimensional system of electromagnetic vortices, called chakras, produces according to definite laws, precise changes to the organs and flesh of everyone of us. The process of the materializing of our subjective states into observable alterations to, for example, the appearance of skin cells will in the future be consciously directed by the individual as the species evolves a new technology of the mind. The supernatural behaviour exhibited by the enlightened mystic, and the paranormal functioning of the body described by the visionary are indicative of the latent potential of each man and woman.

Author's Note

I am deeply indebted to all those who have given their permission to reproduce the quotations and illustrations without which this book could not have been written. Every effort has been made to trace copyright holders, but if any have been inadvertently overlooked, I apologize. Redress will be made in future editions.

Brief descriptions of techniques and exercises will be given in the following chapters. Their inclusion is incidental to my purpose which is to present a general, introductory framework of ideas. Examples of techniques and exercises are provided only in so far as they relate to this overriding purpose, and are not therefore presented with sufficient information for their safe and practical use. The reader should not attempt their practice, but refer instead to the books mentioned within the text and listed in the bibliography.

The content of this book is not intended as a substitute for proper medical advice. Neither I, nor my publishers, can accept responsibility for injuries or illness arising out of a failure by readers to take the advice of a competent physician.

Night Vision

CHAPTER ONE

Kundalini

Here in the West, scientists are debating the possibilities of biotechnology. There is growing confidence in the power of genetics to arrest the ageing process, and the expectation that within a generation the disease of ageing will be eradicated. So what, if anything, has the East to contribute to this debate? An expert on the East, Dr. Paul Brunton, in his book *The Quest of the Overself*, writes:

> We Westerners are rightly proud of our achievements in face-lifting this world of ours, but we get a little disturbed sometimes when we hear of a half-naked fakir performing a feat which we can neither match nor understand. The thing keeps on occurring sufficiently often to remind us that there are ancient secrets and hoary wisdom in the lands which lie East of Suez, and that the inhabitants of those colourful countries are not all the benighted heathens some of us think they are. We picture these yogis as dreaming enthusiasts who desert the normal ways of mankind to go off into strange hiding-places, into gloomy caves, lonely mountains and secluded forests. But they go off with a clear objective, setting themselves no less a task than the acquisition of a perfect and incredible control over the

frail tenement of flesh. To attain this end they practise the hard and exacting discipline laid down in their traditions. *

These traditions are apparently of little interest to Western scientists. Indeed Romain Rolland in his book *Prophets of the New India* writes:

> It is astonishing that Western reason has taken so little into account the experimental research of Indian Raja yogins, and that it has not tried to use the methods of control and mastery, which they offer in broad daylight without any mystery, over the one infinitely fragile and constantly warped instrument that is our only means of discovering what exists.

The 'warped instrument' is of course the human body. Just how accomplished are these Raja-yogins? What evidence of longevity is there? In his book *Teach Yourself Yoga*, James Hewitt writes:

> Great ages are reached in the Yoga ashrams of the East, where lives of self-mastery and tranquillity are lived. Exact figures are difficult to obtain, but claims of up to two hundred years are made. In China, where meditation is an ancient art, the Taoists lived such long lives that the Emperor Ch-Hoang-Ti thought they must have a secret elixir and sent for it.

So what is Yoga? Yoga is more than a physical fitness programme. It involves a sort of mental technology that has been almost unheard of in the West. As children, as adults, throughout our lives, we've been expected to see the world through the eyes of Science. It is perhaps more easy to spot religious fundamentalism

---

* Dr. Paul Brunton, *The Quest Of The Overself* (York Beach, ME: Samuel Weiser, 1970) p. 13. Reproduced by permission.

in distant lands than in our own. Science, Technology, is God for many people in the West. And I was not too surprised to hear a television celebrity recently denounce as 'blasphemy' the suggestion that the physical universe may be no more than the illusion described by older civilisations.

For the yogi, the practitioner of Yoga, the mind is the ultimate piece of technology with which to manipulate physical experience. Yoga provides the theoretical, yet practical framework that eventually, for those few individuals who are sufficiently adept, makes possible the direct manipulation of physical phenomena through mental exercise. In other words, once the basic illusory nature of physical experience is realised, then that illusion may be manipulated at mental levels, with events being edited in and out by the enlightened individual. And the age and appearance of your body can be selected.

We are used to thinking of the future as gradually evolving. But perhaps a case can be made for more sudden changes to human experience. It is being argued by reputable people that there may be an almost hidden agenda for the species, that the control over his environment exhibited by the yogi may become the accepted norm for human behaviour, with all its implications. It would be as if we have, in the past, been aware only of the last word of each sentence, with our science trying to make sense of this lack of data. Then, by the opening up of our consciousness, we begin to perceive the rest of those sentences. As competence in dreaming, and a recognition of what dreams are, develops, we will some day remember a time when events happened to us, out of the blue, and shudder.

In Yoga, dreaming is not something that happens in your sleep; rather it involves the precise re-focusing of waking consciousness in the dream universe. It is about turning our attention inwards, away from the physical, and is achieved through meditation. Put simply:

dreams are a meeting-place where you meet the higher self or Spirit that oversees your life. Dreaming therefore leads to enlightenment, which is experienced when normal consciousness is merged with the consciousness of the higher self. This merging of consciousness, or 'union', which is what the word Yoga means, results in the generation of a new faculty of perception.

The yogi now perceives with the all-seeing 'third eye'. Located in the centre of the forehead between the physical eyes, the third eye is formed out of pre-physical energies, and is therefore invisible. Third eye vision means that the yogi is able to 'see' beyond the range of scientific instruments. He perceives energy in its pre-physical state, and through the directing power of the third eye, he directs its transformation into the physical energies that form matter.

Our bodies seen by those with third eye vision are bodies of light, which flash and whirl with rainbow colours, becoming to the physical senses the rippling muscular surface of the athlete's physique. Empty space is flooded with this pre-physical light which is to be here and there focused into form, into the scenes of history, of gravity, to be pondered upon by the weighty intellect, only to be whisked away from our perception, back into the light.

Our bodies of light, which are composed of pre-physical energy, are called 'energy bodies' and exist within a luminous energy field. The chakras of the energy body are those vortices of electrical energy which are of particular interest to anyone wishing to use the third eye to control the appearance of the body. There are seven key chakras located along the spinal axis from the base of the spine to the top of the head. Key because the way energy flows through the chakral system determines whether or not the third eye is functioning.

To summarize: during human evolution, our consciousness, our energy is concentrated first in the lower chakras. As our nature

1   The Chakras

becomes less emotional, more mental and then more spiritual, our energy is concentrated up into the higher chakras, where it is re-united with the descending energy of the higher self. There is interaction between these increasingly energised chakras, and an overlapping of their energies. A new vortex results and with it third eye vision. This vision will allow men and women to perceive the underlying structures of reality, to control appearances from the inside out. Historically we are at a time when the use of the third eye is to become more widespread. So it is written in books that do not as yet reach western classrooms. The energy body is the prephysical version of the physical body; its blueprint. And the yogi, using his third eye, perceives the energy body and can make changes to it which are then reflected in the physical body. He has two possibilities. He can either instantaneously replace an ageing body with a younger one, or, working through the usual processes, he can bring about gradual changes to his physical appearance. His knowledge tells him which physical glands correspond to the chakras of the energy body, and he may therefore direct energy through the energy body to stimulate activity in the hormonal sys-tem – hormones being those messengers of the physical body whose activity varies so within a given lifespan, and whose activity switches genes on and off. He chooses to override the 'natural' pat-terns of bodily behaviour. He may choose to rejuvenate his body.

Whereas science deals with the natural laws of the known uni-verse, the yogi concerns himself with nature's source. He finally achieves the perception and control of the pre-physical version of matter. He understands that as water vapour condenses to ice, so the pre-physical condenses to be perceived by the physical senses. He learns how to materialise and dematerialise his body at will.

Of course the streets of India are not teeming with people who are this accomplished. The idea is that the average man or woman

2 The overlapping of the chakras induces third eye vision

3   *The Third Eye is located in the centre of the forehead, between the physical eyes*

in the street is now sufficiently evolved that in this New Age which is supposedly upon us, the Age of Aquarius, with its precise cosmic ray influences, he or she could make the leap, inherit the future, become god-like . . . .

It is surprisingly the holy men of India who state that it is the return of Christ that will clinch all this. Perhaps to have taken reality at face value, as we have in the West, will prove to be one of History's better jokes.

There is now much talk about virtual reality, and about the projection of holograms that appear real. And there is the growing belief among physicists that Life is basically just that; holographic. In fact there is now a strange alliance forming between some physicists and those who would advocate a more mystical understanding of existence.

They believe that 'cause and effect' is just one of the ways of organizing experience, to be used for a time, according to our understanding of reality, and to be discarded once physical appearances are known to be holographic, virtual, dreamlike . . . Reality will then be manipulated as easily as the environments of our dreams, with whole scenes appearing and disappearing according to the whim of the dreamer. And, as with our dreams, we will choose the appearance of our bodies.

Before discussing this consensus, it is of interest to note that reference is made to the third eye, also known as the single eye, in the Christian Bible, in Luke's Gospel:

> The light of the body is the eye: therefore when thine eye be single thy whole body shall be full of light.

And it is understood that the Magi, or, translated, the Magicians, used their inner vision to locate the baby Jesus. Curiously, Indian records show Jesus as having been in India for a while during his last incarnation.

4   *In Lewis Carroll's book* Through The Looking-Glass, *Alice climbs through the looking-glass and jumps down into an identical room that exists somehow in reflected space. In a holographic universe, all experience of space is illusory.*

CHAPTER TWO

Origins

The idea that physical existence may, after all, be 'maya' or the illusion of Eastern tradition is being taken seriously by greater numbers of physicists and neurophysiologists, among them Nobel prizewinners, who have developed over recent years the Holographic Model of the Universe described by Michael Talbot in his book, *The Holographic Universe*.

To read that, David Bohm, the physicist Einstein thought with, believed the universe to be holographic . . . This staggers those of us whose exposure to physics at school was strictly orthodox. Have we been left behind with the flat-earthers with our commonsensical view of reality? Certainly the idea that the body's appearance is the result of holographic projection defies common-sense. Yet such talk would not raise an eyebrow in the ashrams of the East where the illusory nature of appearance has been recognized for many thousands of years.

That existence may indeed be holographic is suggested by research into the brain, and the failure of physics to explain the interconnectedness of sub-atomic behaviour – the apparently instantaneous communication that takes place between subatomic particles, and the failure of any other model of reality to explain the paranormal.

The commonsensical notion that a particular memory should have a particular location in the brain has been disproved by research which has shown that memory is distributed 'non-locally'; that a memory has no specific location in the brain, but instead each location seems to hold all memories, so that, for example, when a man has damaged a portion of his brain in an accident, he does not lose a proportion of his memory. And when the brain of a salamander has been minced and then squeezed back inside its skull, the salamander carries on normally.

Research at Indiana University has shown that the brain of the salamander may be removed and replaced without killing it. The salamander remains in a stupor while the brain is missing. This fact was used by the biologist Paul Pietsch to test the idea that memories have no specific location. He reasoned that if the salamander's memory of how to eat has no specific location, then a change in the brain's position in the salamander's head would not affect its eating.

First he flip-flopped the left and right hemispheres of the salamander's brain, but it had no effect. Then he turned the brain of another salamander upside down. No effect. Over 700 operations followed, with the brain being sliced, flipped, shuffled, subtracted and minced; all with no effect.

The visual system is also strange in its operation. The well-received belief that the eye delivers a photographic-like, electrically coded image to the brain which remarkably turns it into a full-blown picture of reality has, it seems, been disproved by research. If, for example, 90% of a rat's visual cortex is surgically excised (the visual cortex is the outer layer of the brain that receives information from the eyes), the rat continues to see the 'whole picture', performing complex tasks. The same is true when the optic nerve connecting the retina behind the eyeball with the brain is almost totally severed. When researchers sought to explain how this could be, they found that visual information is processed and stored using holographic mathematics.

Holographic film projects a virtual image called a hologram: virtual because it creates the illusion of a three-dimensional object in space. This film, because of the mathematics used in recording information on its surface, looks very different from normal camera film. You don't see a positive or negative image of the object photographed, but instead a blur of 'interference patterns' that reminds you of a pond's surface when a handful of stones is tossed in, and the surface is rippling with small waves (see diagram p. 17). These interference patterns result from the interference of light-waves that are reflected from the object being photographed onto the surface of holographic film. The mathematics involved was thought of by a Frenchman called Fourier in the eighteenth century. Because of it, a piece of holographic film can be cut in half, and you don't just see half a hologram. You don't just see the top half of someone's body projected, for example, but the legs as well. Holographic mathematics means you can take a piece of holographic film, cut it into smaller and smaller pieces, and each fragment will project the whole hologram. This is not true, however, of the type of holographic film whose images are visible to the naked eye.

Research has shown that if plaid and checkerboard patterns are 'translated' using Fourier's mathematics, and these translations are presented to the visual cortex, the brain cells clearly respond to this holographic data. So the visual system must be processing information using holographic mathematics. This discovery was made in 1979 by Berkeley neurophysiologists Russell and Karen De Valois, and has been repeatedly confirmed in laboratories around the world.

Once this result was known to Karl Pribram, the

neurophysiologist who has been working with Bohm, he was struck by the possibility that perhaps there are no objects out there in space. He reasoned that the space seemingly occupied by objects, and the empty space between objects is filled with waves, and the brain uses the interference patterns of these oscillating waves to project a hologram of the body and its environment. Pribram called this universe of oscillating waves the 'frequency domain'*. The brain is itself a part of the frequency domain, and like the rest of the body is composed of interference patterns.

The Nobel Prize-winner and physiologist Georg von Bekesy has investigated the way the brain projects the sensation of touch. By varying the frequencies of the vibrators he places on the knees of blindfolded test subjects, he makes them feel that a point source of vibration is jumping from knee to knee. More than this, he has made his subjects feel a point source in the space between the knees. In other words, he has shown that the human brain can project sensation to a location where the body has no sense receptors. In the same way, when the brain receives information from the frequency domain about the objects we touch, it projects the sensation so that we experience it at our fingertips.

Physicists have been developing their Holographic Model in recent years. At one time it was thought that quantum physics provided a full explanation of how reality works, but now it is being thought there may be this frequency domain which is being compared with the eastern idea that 'All Is Vibration'. Borrowing from Yoga, physicists describe the frequency domain as being multi-levelled. This means that the interference patterns that form physical space at any time and which our brains overlay with holographic

---

* Frequency is the measure of the number of oscillations a wave undergoes per second; its rate of vibration

5　*A piece of holographic film showing the interference patterns*
(Illustration from Understanding Holography *by Michael Wenyon.*
Reproduced by permission.)

projections originate in the pre-physical levels of the frequency domain. As a result, changes made in these other levels are reflected in the physical universe. Specifically, changes made to the interference patterns of the energy body are reflected in the interference patterns of the physical body. The chakras of the energy body are part of its structure of interference patterns.

Yoga's energy field is thought to be the human version of the frequency domain. Mental images form patterns in the pre-physical levels of the energy field, and the process of their materialization can be observed. Emanuel Swedenborg, born in 1688, and Sweden's answer to the greats of the Italian Renaissance, being a mathematician, physicist, chemist, astronomer, and inventor, claimed to be able to see people's imaginings 'condensing' in the energy field. And he reported seeing people's thoughts and images in the 'wave-substance' that he perceived as enveloping the human body. Explaining his ability he said: 'I could see solid concepts of thought as though they were surrounded by a kind of wave. But nothing reaches human sensation except what is in the middle and seems solid.'

Michael Talbot describes modern examples of psychics who have the ability to see 'three-dimensional movies' or holograms in a person's energy field. Most well-known is Carol Dryer, who also sees the energy field in terms of waves of energy. She is able to 'telescope' her vision through the levels and dimensions of the energy field, and reports seeing kaleidoscopic clouds of light, gossamer mists and glistening shapes.

Orthodox medical science is incapable of providing any satisfactory explanation as to why the use of mental imagery by, for example, cancer patients can yield results, improving life expectancy. But in a holographic universe we can select the body's interference patterns by the use of the imagination; by visualisation.

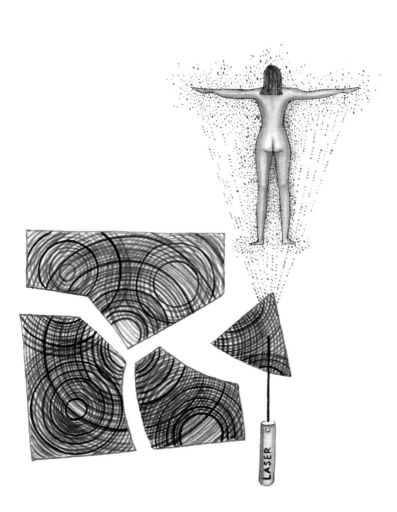

6   *Each piece of holographic film projects the whole image*

In a test in Russia, four groups of Olympic athletes trained using a mixture of physical exercise and visualisation in these proportions – 100% physical; 75% physical, 25% visualisation; 50% physical, 50% visualisation; and 25% physical, 75% visualisation. In the Winter games at Lake Placid, New York, the fourth group performed best.

That visualisation works is suggested by some research into Multiple Personality Disorder. The sub personalities of a Multiple operate independently of each other. When one personality is in control, the other sub-personalities are still aware. This explains why Multiples heal faster than the rest of us. It is possible to have a sub-personality whose function is the 24 hour visualisation of the body. And Doctor Cornelia Wilbur, who has been studying the condition, believes that Multiples do not age as fast.

In Tibet, so seriously was the potential of the imagination taken that some mystics practised visualisation to an extreme degree. Monks of the Kargyupa sect spent up to seven years in solitude, sealed in a room, perfecting their visualisation, and thereby developing third-eye vision.

More insight into the holographic production of reality was achieved in 1972 by Harvard vision researchers Daniel Pollen and Michael Tractenberg who were making a study of the mechanics of photographic memory. Individuals with photographic memory, wishing to recall a scene from the past, project a mental image of it onto a screen or blank wall. In the study, a Harvard art history professor perceived her projected images with almost total clarity. And after scanning a page from Goethe's Faust and projecting her image of it out into space, she read the page with her eyes moving as if reading a real page. The next stage or level of control would obviously be to have your private projections perceived by others.

There is the case of Sai Baba, living in the state of Andhra

EMANUEL SWEDENBORG.
Affesfour of the Royal Metallic College in the
KINGDOM of SWEDEN.

7   Emanuel Swedenborg (1688–1772)

Pradesh in southern India. He is said to materialize whatever object is requested of him, and he has been doing this for half a century in front of scientists, magicians, cameras and crowds of thousands. He can, for example, materialize a composite fruit, half apple and half something else. All this has been studied for over ten years by the psychologist, Erlendur Haraldsson, who believes Sai Baba's demonstrations reveal 'the enormous potentials that may lie dormant somewhere within all human beings.' Numerous witnesses have reported seeing Sai Baba snap his fingers, vanish, and reappear a hundred or more yards away.

When biologist and investigator of the paranormal, Lyall Watson, author of Supernature, chanced upon the Indonesian shaman Tia talking to a girl in the shade of kenari trees, he was witness to a direct, controlled, manipulation of the holographic environment. Keeping his distance, he saw Tia begin her shamanistic dance. She then gestured towards the trees. Watson insists that Tia caused the grove of kenari trees to disappear and reappear, causing the holographic projection to blink on and off. Each time the trees were gone, Tia and the girl would be standing alone in bright sunlight.

Another example of blatant holographic activity is the case of Indridi Indridason, the Icelandic medium. In 1905 he was investigated by leading Icelandic scientists. In deep trance, an arm or a hand would disappear, dematerialized, only to reappear in front of these startled onlookers.

And finally there is the now famous case of the two Oxford professors, Anne Moberly, the principal of St. Hugh's College, and Eleanor Jourdain, the vice-principal, who were taking a walk through the garden of the Petit Trianon at Versailles in the summer of 1901. With academic rigour they had been observing the correct normality of the scene. Then, all of a sudden, the afternoon light

8   *Anne Moberly*

9   *Eleanor Jourdain*

shimmered over a landscape that faded and dissolved in front of them. And they were surprised to find themselves in a new garden; a garden which was crowded with men in wigs. It was the eighteenth century. A man with a pock-marked face ran up to them and begged them to follow him past a line of trees to a garden where stood the elegant figure of perhaps Marie Antoinette painting a watercolour.

When the music stopped and the scene was again 1901, the two professors set off to research eighteenth century Versailles, and later became convinced that they had walked into the afternoon of the massacre of the Swiss Guards and the sacking of the Tuileries. Their book-length manuscript describing the adventure is with the British Society for Psychical Research, which also has records of similar occurrences at Versailles.

Before looking at the experience of the Yaqui Indians, it is of interest that both Samuel Taylor Coleridge and William Blake attempted to reveal holographic Nature in their mystical poetry. Coleridge described the frequency domain:

And what if all of animated nature
Be but organic harps, diversely framed,
That tremble into thought, as o'er them sweeps
Plastic and vast, one intelligible breeze,
At once the soul of each, and God of All?

And Blake, in his poem, Auguries of Innocence, reveals the within-ness of Nature:

To see a World in a grain of sand
And a Heaven in a wild flower,
Hold Infinity in the palm of your hand
And Eternity in an hour.

10   William Blake (1757–1827)

CHAPTER THREE

Shamanism

The writer Carlos Castaneda met don Juan Matus, a Yaqui Indian sorcerer, in 1961 when he was a graduate student of anthropology at the University of California. As part of his university work, Carlos Castaneda was assessing the usefulness of the medicinal plants of the Yaqui Indians of Mexico, specifically *Datura inoxia*, *Lophorphora williamsii* and a plant of the genus *Psilocybe*. He did not suspect that they were being used for their holographic properties. And when confronted by the effects produced by the ingestion of these plants, he was convinced that he had experienced the most vivid hallucinations. But he was to change his mind. The plants were being used to move something called the 'assemblage point' in the human energy field.

According to don Juan, there is a vast number of threads or filaments of light within the energy field. But only a smaller number of them are brightly lit at any time. They are lit up by a point of intense brilliance called the assemblage point. This assemblage point may be moved to a new position within the energy field. And when the assemblage point is moved, there is a change to the perceived reality. For example, it takes a minute shifting of the assemblage point to produce immediate rejuvenation. It takes a greater movement to perceive other worlds.

All this would have been considered bizarre were it not for the development of the holographic view of perception. Quoted by Michael Talbot and many academics, the accounts of Carlos Castaneda's experiences with don Juan are being taken seriously. Remember the holographic idea that, just as every fragment of a piece of holographic film contains the information of the whole, there is hidden within any point in space the entire experience of the Universe, past, present and future. Don Juan did not, for example, have to physically travel from A to B; a controlled movement of the assemblage point would wipe away one reality to replace it with whatever reality was projected by the newly-lit conglomeration of light filaments. An involuntary movement of this assemblage point would of course explain the reappearance of eighteenth century Versailles in the summer of 1901.

It seems the aim of the Yaqui sorcerers is ambitious: to achieve a state of awareness, of consciousness, that allows for the experience of all the possibilities of perception available. These possibilities include experience in human and non-human realms: physical living may be something of a rarity in the Universe. It is superfluous to add that these people do not die normally, but merely move their assemblage points away from earthly frequencies, so disappearing from our perception. And unless your assemblage point is in the same position in your energy field as it is in someone else's you do not perceive the same reality. So it is possible for whole populations to tune into new worlds by the movement of the assemblage point away from the normal energy band.

Don Juan argues that, for humanity to survive, we must revive our knowledge of the assemblage point. Most people of course are unaware that there is more to perception than the day to day experience that is projected when the assemblage point is at normal positions.

SHAMANISM

The apprentice sorcerer learns control over the movement of the assemblage point, and how to fix it in a new position so that precise changes are made to perception. The force that moves the assemblage point for him is known as the Spirit. There is available to each of us a communication link with this force, but the closest the average man or woman gets to activating this link is the experience of that higher faculty; intuition. This is to be developed, writes Carlos Castaneda, by the 'cleaning of the link', into direct knowing or 'silent knowledge'. Direct knowing is knowing something without knowing how you know it. This knowing, like 'seeing', happens when contact with the Spirit is established.

Not for a long time, according to don Juan, has the majority of humankind been aware that such a communication link exists. He suggests that the Garden of Eden story of the Christian Bible is really about the time long ago when the assemblage point moved from the general position of silent knowledge, of knowledge of the Spirit, to the position of reason. These general positions of the assemblage point relate to the movement of energy in the chakral system, as consciousness changes its focus. The seven chakras of Yoga are recognised and referred to by the Yaqui Indians as the 'seven ancestral villages'. And, as with Yoga, the purpose of the Yaquis is to reverse the descent into isolation described in the Bible.

To re-establish his link with the Spirit, the apprentice sorcerer is trained in the disciplines of the 'Warrior's path'. This personal struggle was undertaken by Carlos Castaneda in his thirteen year apprenticeship with don Juan from 1961 to 1974.

The apprentice learns to lose 'self-importance', and therefore conserves the energy that would otherwise be used in maintaining his position in society. And he further conserves his energy by learning to live 'impeccably'. Living in this way means following a code of behaviour that requires sobriety, frugality and simplicity. The apprentice therefore redirects his energy away from normal interaction towards the Spirit.

A conscious effort is made to relate to the world differently by avoiding routine patterns of behaviour that correspond to regular changes to the position of the assemblage point. It is called 'not-doing', and its purpose is to break up the continuity that we experience when the assemblage point is at the general position of reason. It is about viewing the world through almost alien eyes, pretending that you're trying hard to make any sense at all, and deliberately making new, irrational connections about reality. The result is that the assemblage point moves from the general position of reason to the position of silent knowledge, and the apprentice sorcerer finds himself in communication with the Spirit. As with Yoga, this is reflected in the chakral system by the generation of the third eye vortex. Through this vortex, the sorcerer communicates his intent to rejuvenate his body, for example, direct to the Spirit. And the Spirit responds by shifting the assemblage point to a position that projects a rejuvenated body.

And through the third eye, the sorcerer 'sees' the position of the assemblage point, and perceives the different realities contained in the different positions of the assemblage point. Over thousands of years, the Yaqui sorcerers have recorded the results of moving the assemblage point to a vast number of different positions. Dreaming, or the 'Art of Dreaming' is used to try out new positions. If a new environment is projected by a certain movement of the assemblage point, and the sorcerer wishes to experience this reality physically, he fixes the assemblage point at the new position. His physical body is as a result 'pulled' after his dream body through the vortex into the chosen reality. There has, however, to be sufficient energy to 'tip the scales', or the dream body will instead be pulled back to the location of his physical body*.

As India has its deathless guru, the ever-youthful Babaji, so the Yaqui Indians have their Death Defier, a sorcerer of ancient times who admits to being several thousand years old, and who survives by her control of the assemblage point. Originally a man with his assemblage point in the male position, the Death Defier prefers to be female. According to don Juan, the male position has the shiniest part of the assemblage point facing inwards, and the female position has the shiniest part facing outwards.

The Death Defier's power of visualization is so developed that she is able to visualize the details of an entire dream-town which is projected out by a corresponding movement of the assemblage point. She comments to Carlos Castaneda as they stroll together through the streets of her dream that the people who populate her creation even have their own thoughts. By imagining the details of a physical town, and by reproducing it as a dream, the sorcerers of ancient times could jointly materialize an identical town 'elsewhere', as concrete and as real as the original town.

Babaji also is reported to have materialized a golden palace upon the snows of the Himalayan mountains.

---

* During dreaming , the energy body separates into the dream body and the 'etheric' body, each with its own set of chakras. The etheric body, which is referred to in the Bible as the 'golden bowl', remains within the physical body. When the dream is over, the three bodies operate again as a unit, with the chakras of the dream body being re-aligned with the chakras of the etheric body. The dream body is also referred to as the astral body.

CHAPTER FOUR

Paganism

Djwhal Khul, the Tibetan Master, reminds us that there is a Plan for the Universe, and that it has been the purpose of Christ and the Buddha, amongst others, to guide us into the future. It is not of course necessary for a highly developed personality to physically incarnate to make his or her teaching known. It is also possible for information to be 'channelled' through someone who is living.

The personality of Seth*, or Setekh as he was also known to the Ancient Egyptians, began speaking through the body of Jane Roberts in the sixties. Jane Roberts was the American mystic featured in Time magazine, who had regular meetings with physicists. In the seventies and eighties, she produced a number of 'Seth books'.

In *The Nature of Personal Reality*, Seth refers to the practicality of dreaming, the importance of the imagination, the importance of the emotions, and the use of emotional intensity in the acceleration of mental imagery into matter. And he suggests that there are

---

*   Seth was, according to the 'priestly' tradition, the first-born son of Adam and Eve. Seth is more prominent in the Jewish tradition than in the Old Testament. He was 'glorified'. There was also a Jewish sect known as the Sethites, whose doctrines were taken over by a Christian gnostic sect. To the Ancient Egyptians he was a god.

11   Seth (right) as depicted by the Ancient Egyptians, and Horus opposite

definite steps whereby mental imagery is transformed into matter, and that all but the tail-end of this process of materialisation lies beyond the scope of scientific instruments. So science is dealing with the products of our imaginations and does not know it. Further, mental images are developed in the darkroom of our dreams, and it is only by accessing our dreams that we learn to control our physical condition.

The difference between the Yaqui sorcerer, or the Indian Yogi, and ourselves is that our consciousness has not yet evolved to include awareness of the dream universe. We cannot therefore follow our thoughts and images into that universe, and there organise and direct their materialisation. This is the next stage in our evolution, which is as yet only demonstrated by a few advanced men and women.

Most of us in the West have come close to accepting science's view of existence. Rejuvenation, we are told, if possible at all, is to be achieved by the manipulation of the physical fabric, by such things as genetic engineering. Scientists become rather hot under the collar when it is pointed out that a theory such as science's theory of existence, which is repeated *ad nauseam* down through the years, does not become a statement of fact. It still needs to be proven. The theory that there is only the physical universe cannot of course be proven, though some scientists would have you believe otherwise. Scientists confidently expect this theory to be proven soon, very soon, or seem to argue that the longer it remains unrefuted, the more nearly proven the theory becomes.

According to science, human consciousness is the by-product of chance chemical reaction, of evolution. Somewhere in the brain, yet to be located, is you. When the physical matter of your brain 'dies', your existence is over. Your body, according to this hypothesis, is a machine. It is assumed that any real progress in the rejuvenation of the human body will result from a greater understanding of its mechanisms. And so there is great talk of the possibilities of biotechnology as the bringer of new life, and, perhaps, nightmare.

Seth's view of existence, which is in agreement with Eastern tradition, is totally at odds with that of science. He has consciousness evolving matter and not the other way round, with human consciousness being shaped by some greater consciousness to fit the contours of space and time, and with the physical experience of man mirroring the evolution of his consciousness. And, with that evolution comes an endless substitution of beliefs about what is physically possible, and this mental posturing of the species determines what is experienced. The species first imagines the future in line with what is believed about reality, and then experiences that future.

Your brain, he suggests, and its perceptive apparatus is tuned only to physical frequencies because its purpose is to perceive physical phenomena. As a consequence, we make the error of taking the physical to be all-inclusive. And it is our failure to recognise our true position that leaves us forever reacting to events that are served up for us to experience, rather than taking part in the formation of those events. Further, it is only by enlarging our idea of ourselves, by redefining ourselves, that we become aware of latent abilities presently used by the non-physical portions of ourselves on our behalves. These 'inner' selves* are constantly transforming and solidifying our thoughts and images from the dream state, turning them into hard physical fact. The brain is activated. Like some giant searchlight lighting up a city skyline at night, it generates physical phenomena.

---

*   The inner self is equivalent to the higher self or Spirit.

The inner selves are, put simply, the selves into which we are growing. We each evolve through a number of lives, dipping in and out of planetary existence, becoming ever more conscious of the self that created us in time, but exists outside time, until at some point we become self-conscious to a degree that allows for the conscious creation of events. We then take over the event-forming function from the inner self.

In other words, an individual will evolve through incarnations from being someone who simply reacts to physical stimuli, from being someone who reacts to events seemingly thrust upon him or her by a soulless Darwinian Universe, from a position of victim, to the position of co-creator. We reposition ourselves, changing our relationship with the inner self, and from this new perspective learn to participate in event selection.

Seth refers to the physical universe with its time structure as being a training system, where we are prepared for experience in more advanced realities, in which the experience of time, for example, is simultaneous. Through history, the inner self teaches the physical self how to handle creativity. The inner self is of course aware of the themes of history and the ideas prevalent at any time. So the individual is inserted into the historical slot that provides him or her with the right medium for development. At some point in human history, information is inserted that will allow men and women to glimpse the greater possibilities available. There is then a new understanding of how reality works. The connection is made between mental activity and physical experience. And so we move on from generating a confusion of ideas that come back at us, swarming all over us, forming the fabric of our history, to a point where the individual knows what is going to happen and what mental work is required to bring about the chosen event. We begin to select events for ourselves, swaying and dodging between a near infinity of events, so to gain control of our lives.

Speaking to friends about their dreams, there seems to be a certain logic about their increasing involvement in the processes of dreaming, as if they're being invited to take a look behind the scenery. A regular interest in dreams seems to trigger new experiences.

My own interest in dreams was aroused more than a decade ago. I was living in Spain in a hotel by the sea. One night I'd gone to bed as usual when the normally background images of my dreams began to become more real, to take on a greater reality. At some point, and for the briefest time, I became aware of the dream as I am now aware of being awake. I was aware of being both inside and outside the dream. I was performing in the dream, and I was watching my own performance. The dream location then abruptly changed to a courtyard in England, where I was standing in the dark. I then felt an acceleration rather like an aeroplane beginning its take-off. The acceleration was from the base of my spine upwards. Energy was surging through me. I panicked and woke. As I woke, I was aware of and I watched a 'part of myself', rather like a ball of electricity, separating off and accelerating fast out into the black night over the courtyard buildings. Shaken by this episode, I went for a walk in the grounds of the hotel. I was soon wondering about any possible connections that may exist between the state of dreaming and normal living. Hence this book.

Incidentally, when Celia Green, the director of the Institute of Psychophysical Research in Oxford, polled 115 students at Southampton University, she found 19% had experienced being 'out of their bodies'. As had 34% of the Oxford students also questioned. And a 1980 study by Dr. Harvey Irwin at the University of New England in Australia showed 20% of 177 students had experienced being out of their bodies. In fact statistics abound with such evidence. At a meeting of the American Psychiatric Association, it was recognized that out-of-body experiences are common occurrences and was suggested that patients might do as well to see a yogi as a psychiatrist.

It is widely believed that we are at the threshold of an important change to our consciousness, to our perception of ourselves, that the species is verging on an expansion of consciousness that is to bring about a reality in which events are manipulated increasingly at mental levels. It may be that our consciousness goes through many such transitions, each involving the cultivation of new mental habits.

In the decades ahead, it is now argued that there is to be something of a revolution in Western thinking. The space we occupy, the times we live in, will be seen increasingly to be illusory, projections from an inner arena. Perhaps we are going to learn to appreciate dream activity as something other than the rumblings of an unfocused brain. Dreams will be known to have 'real' locations, accessible to humankind connecting hard physical fact with its source. Perhaps the children of the future will learn to focus their personalities in new ways, delving into their dreams to generate new types of experience, understanding experience from the inside out, leaving the old ideas of science far behind. Perhaps they will not age as we do.

Science's view of existence will retreat into mythology to join those other myths that the species uses in its history. Different myths belong to different times. From the perspective of one myth, another myth seems false, because each myth generates its own facts. We have believed in time, that it should behave itself, keeping its moments apart, and not mixing its tenses. With new ideas of time, it will be realised that our evolution operates as much from the future backwards as from the past forwards, that time is simultaneous though our experience of it is piecemeal.

Men's and women's bodies are being freshly recreated in each moment. Whilst we believe otherwise, that the physique we had a moment ago was younger by one moment, and that our bodies age in time, then that will be our experience. Accordingly, if you imagine yourself in a younger body, but at the same time you do not believe in the possibility of rejuvenation, then rejuvenation will be blocked.

This paramount importance of belief is stressed over and over by Seth, precisely because it so profoundly outrages the commonsense of the western mind that has been schooled in the materialism of Science. Seth confirms Christ's teaching about the hypothetical individual who succeeds in suspending his belief about the concreteness of reality. His new, substituted belief, expressed by the imagination, could then be used to move a mountain, or any other item of the environment.

In his book, The Future of the Body, Michael Murphy, the co-founder of the Esalen Institute, lists examples where a change of belief produces remarkable results. A simple belief that proximity to the burial-place of a saint will restore sight is sufficient to bring about the cure. Or, a belief given by a hypnotist to a subject that he or she is becoming sunburnt, or that a heated object is contacting skin, will, by mere suggestion, result in a reddening of the skin and blistering.

During infancy we grow to accept our parents' and society's beliefs about the body and the limits of its functioning. According to Seth, our genes inherit those same beliefs about how the body should perform as it ages. If we substitute these beliefs, then the body will adjust its behaviour in response. Seth sums this up in his book *Dreams, 'Evolution' and Value Fulfillment*: 'ideas alter chromosomes . . . your genetic structure reacts to each thought that you have'. And in *The Nature of Personal Reality* he states that the 'entire body can be regenerated in a way that would be impossible to predict in usual medical terms'.

Our beliefs prevent the inner self from using its great energy to rejuvenate the body in old age. We are faced instead with the results of our beliefs. According to Seth, this materialization of faulty beliefs is all part of the learning process. We are to be made aware of the power of thought.

Given the above that old beliefs block new experience, *The Nature of Personal Reality* includes exercises, involving self-hypnosis, to ensure the substitution of new beliefs for old. We are reminded that since the advent of the Industrial Revolution around 1760, Western culture has been trying to deny the connection between mind and matter, between belief and its materialisation: the reason being an over-reaction to the previous ideas of religion.

Self-hypnosis occurs whenever we have our own undivided attention. By repeating to ourselves, verbally or mentally, a simple statement of a new belief in the possibility of rejuvenation for up to ten minutes, once a day, the belief may become accepted in substitution for the previous disbelief. Then during the rest of the day our imagination begins to work round a belief in rejuvenation. The inner self becomes aware of our change of belief, and the repetition of the statement activates new biological patterns. According to Seth, at least three days are required to give the new belief time to materialize.* We may have to vary the wording of the statement to get it right. We are told not to strain; to be totally relaxed and focused on the statement for the ten minute period.

A variation on this method of belief substitution requires that we wilfully suspend our disbelief in rejuvenation, again for up to

---

* Any reader wishing to try out Seth's ideas should first read the detailed instructions in *The Nature of Personal Reality*.

ten minutes, imagining and feeling that we are rejuvenated. Acting both as hypnotist and subject, we convince ourselves that the belief in rejuvenation, which will in the future be commonplace, is indeed what we believe. If we succeed in this wilful acceptance of a new belief, then within a month, a change in our physical condition will be evident. Seth gives the example of the old man who succeeds in convincing himself through the use of his imagination that he is young again. He succeeds in reactivating his hormonal system, becoming younger.

The potential of the imagination is set out in the following quote by 'Seth Two', who spoke through Jane Roberts on only a few occasions, and whose level of development far exceeds even that of Seth. He is part of the gestalt of consciousness that is behind the formation of the physical universe:

> We want you to realize that though it is hard for us to communicate, we spoke with your race before your race learned language. We gave you mental images, and upon these images you learned to form the world that you know.
>
> We gave you the patterns, intricate, involved and blessed, from which you form the reality of each physical thing you know. The most minute cell within your brain has been made from the patterns of consciousness which we have given you. We gave you the pattern upon which you formed your entire physical universe . . . and the comprehension that exists within each cell, the knowledge that each cell has, the desire for organization, was given by us. The entire webwork was initiated by us. We taught you to form the reality that you know.

As with Yoga, Seth describes the body as being the outside structure superimposed on an invisible pattern or blueprint composed of inner light, inner sound and electromagnetic properties.

Mental images also have this electromagnetic reality. In fact, mental images are to be understood as 'incipient matter', which exists at first in the realm of dreams and is later fully materialized.

This reflection of mental activity in the physical world is described in the writings of Paramahansa Yogananda, the Indian yogi who introduced the ideas of Yoga to a new audience in the West when he founded the Self-Realization Fellowship in America in 1920. In his *Autobiography of a Yogi*, he states that the world is nothing but an 'objectivised dream'. And in *Man's Eternal Quest*, he explains the power of concentrated visualisation to materialize thought. Intense belief focused by a powerful mind will, according to Paramahansa Yogananda, instantly generate its counterpart in physical experience.

Djwhal Khul emphasizes this power of mind in his *Treatise on Cosmic Fire*:

> Any idea of enough strength will inevitably materialise in dense physical matter . . . The dense physical response is automatic and inevitable.

What the imagination can do, when in the hands of an expert, is described by J. H. Brennan in his *Astral Projection Workbook*. The expert was Alexandra David-Neel, who lived in pre-invasion Tibet, and was perhaps the only woman ever to be made a 'lama'.

In Tibetan tradition, a tulpa is an entity created by the imagination, by the prolonged and intensive use of the imagination. Experimenting, Alexandra David-Neel visualized a new companion, a plump benign monk. At first he had his existence somewhere in her imagination. However, with practice she succeeded in projecting her ghostly monk out into the real world. But still she was the only person who could perceive him. Gradually she was able to give him greater reality. And whenever she wished, she could

12   Alexandra David-Neel

43

project his appearance. Until the day came when her monk decided that this intermittent existence was not for him. He refused to remain forever under her control. Now he sometimes appeared when not invited and was soon changing his appearance. He lost weight and seemed almost sinister. And then one day Alexandra David-Neel's physical companions enquired about the stranger in their midst. They had been unaware that she was experimenting with the tulpa creation.

CHAPTER FIVE

Dreams

Our thoughts and mental images have their primary existence within the dream universe. A new body image, for example, is first tried out in our dreams, and, if conditions of intensity and belief are met, the etheric and physical bodies are activated to reproduce that image.

We have a choice. We can visualize a future event or physical condition, and then wait to see whether our efforts at visualization have the quality required to realize that future. In other words, we start the ball rolling from the waking state, and hope and pray for physical results some time later. Or we can enter our dreams and try to guide their physical outcome.

The literature on dreaming is substantial, and the experts advise us to keep a record of our dreams. The idea is to write down or speak into a recorder as much as we remember of our dreams immediately we wake up. Two refinements are that you wake yourself up at various times in the night to try to record the different stages of the dreaming process, and, secondly, there is the possibility of recording your dreams without waking up. This is done through self-suggestion.

The dream record provides us with an appreciation of our dreams so that when we find ourselves suddenly awake within the dream state, there is familiarity. For example, some dreams deal with the more personal matters, such as our physical condition, and others rehearse the 'mass events' that the species will experience. And when these mass dreams are translated into physical fact, each participant perceives only his own projections.

Intact within your waking recollection may be the memory of your dreaming self projecting out of the dream universe and into one of those worlds that are dream generated. There are also 'objective' areas of the dream universe; realms that you may be drawn to, according to your state of mind. Djwhal Khul refers to dream reality as being the playground of the gods.

People often have vague, waking memories of faces and places in their dreams that turn up later in their lives. These memories appear jumbled and chaotic. For there in our dreams time is whenever we want it to be, and it therefore does not give us that sense of continuity which we rely on to provide a framework for physical experience. For example, you may be talking to a friend in a dream who happens to live next door to you in real life, and, in mid-sentence, he is substituted by a young girl who is in fact another incarnation of your friend. So one moment you are looking into the eyes of an adult, and the next you are looking into the eyes of a perhaps equally startled young girl. Your surprise grows when an almost identical girl appears on the scene; until you realise that she is a 'probable self' of the first girl who lives physically at different frequencies in a parallel world. Then a second version of your adult friend taps you on the shoulder and you realise that his first dream form was in fact your own subconscious projection.

The scenes of our dreams will often include incongruous elements that belong to different historical periods. Unwelcome elements of our private dreams can be willed away. Nightmares too can be banished, or perhaps studied for insights into the state of our psyches. This study of dreams will reveal our own unique use of dream symbolism. Symbols are the psychic shorthand that give meaning to our dreams. For example, a belief in evil may be projected in the form of demons who scare us until we realise their symbolism.

We are warned not to visit our dreams in a pessimistic frame of mind. That negativity can energize and give form to a lower-dimensional 'creature' which confronts the dreamer in his or her first moments outside the physical body. There is panic when instead this scary creature, a being of our own inner creation, may be willed away with such words as 'May peace be with you'.

Similar creations by others exist as 'potential forms' that can be plucked from the frequency domain and given form by the energy of our attention. The nature of the forms encountered, whether pleasant or not, is again determined by our frame of mind. Withdrawing attention causes these forms to disappear back into the underlying reality.

If you find yourself awake in a dream that is alarming, you always have the option of willing yourself back into the physical body. There is a 'cord' which connects your dream to your physical body which is only 'cut' when you die*. The dream body feels physical and it is only when you try to use it physically that you

---

* The 'Silver Cord', which is referred to in the Bible, transmits a record of dreams to the physical body via the etheric body. Connecting a chakra in the dream body to its equivalent in the etheric body, this cord is 'infinitely elastic', allowing the dream body which is usually coincident with the physical and etheric bodies to separate and to travel vast distances in the solar system and to enter dream space. The dream body, also called the astral body, is normally invisible.

realise that you are not in your usual body. This is why people who have just died are often frantically trying to communicate the fact that they are still alive to their relatives. It is the body that you use between lives while you are still incarnating within the physical system.

As the physical self or 'outer ego' is the part of the whole self that surfaces to experience the outer world, so the inner self or 'inner ego' surfaces in the dream universe. This inner ego is the 'I' of our dreams, being both the director of our dreams and the selector of those dream events that we physically experience. In terms of frequency, the connecting reality of dreams exists between the 'natural' environments of the inner and outer egos. So the inner ego is based on the 'far side' of our dreams at a level of reality beyond space and time. This is why the time we experience in our dreams is so different. It is in a sense a bastard species of time that exists between the no-time condition found at frequencies beyond our dreams, and physical time with its strict chronological order.

When the outer ego learns to emerge fully conscious in the dream state, contact between the two egos becomes possible. Seth likens this meeting of minds to the situation that can happen when you get talking to a stranger on a train, and find out that you're really not strangers at all. This is then followed by the gradual merging of the egos. The outer ego or self enlarges the scope of his or her activities, and begins to take a hand in the direction of dreams, becoming involved in the selection process, and deciding, for example, his or her physical appearance.

The Victorian poet, Robert Browning, in his book *Paracelsus,* wrote:

Such men are even now upon the earth,
Serene amid the half-formed creatures round.

13   Robert Browning (1812–1889)

For men begin to pass their nature's bound,
And find new hopes and cares which fast supplant
Their proper joys and grief; they grow too great
For narrow creeds of right and wrong.

These men and women may well have joined that esoteric Victorian Order known as the Golden Dawn, and practised something called the Body of Light Technique. With this technique the dream body is projected by the use of the imagination from the waking state.

J. H. Brennan describes how it is done. You relax in a chair in a room where you will not be disturbed. And then you imagine yourself standing in front of the chair about six feet away. This visualization has to be as detailed as you can make it, and Brennan advises ten to fifteen minutes a day to be set aside for what is really the exercising of invisible mental muscles : 'just don't devote more than, say, twenty minutes each day to the practice: this is more than enough, so long as you practise regularly'. Once you reach the point when you can call up or will the appearance of this version of yourself standing there in front of you, move on to 'phase two' of the technique.

In phase two, you imagine yourself getting up from the chair, and slowly moving about your room. So before you close your eyes, you must have an exact knowledge of the room so that from any imagined perspective you know what you're trying to visualize. After a time the effort required for this exercise in continuous visualization diminishes.

For the final phase, you again visualize your dream body standing six feet away. You hold that image steady. Then you attempt to look out through your dream body's eyes. After a number of attempts, which Brennan likens to learning to ride a bicycle, you may suddenly succeed. You will be looking straight at your seated physical body. You then try to repeat your imagined walk around the room. If your consciousness flickers back to your physical body, you try again to project it into your dream body. Then, according to Brennan, one of two things happens. Either gradually or suddenly the sense of reality of this new experience increases until you are fully conscious and perceiving clearly.

Though initially you may find yourself in the dream body in normal surroundings, its natural environment is the dream environment. There is then the opportunity of locating those areas of the dream world where the selection of physical events is made.

The use of sound as a means of achieving out-of-body consciousness is being researched under laboratory conditions at the Monroe Institute in Virginia. Its founder Robert Monroe and a team of biochemists have developed 'Hemi-Sync', a state-of-the-art audio technology, which both synchronizes and amplifies the electrical activity of the brain. Complex sound patterns have been identified that induce consciousness of the dream state.

Monroe invites the readers of his book, *Ultimate Journey,* to participate in the Gateway programs at the Institute. The 'Gateway Voyage' is a six-day program that uses the hemi-sync frequency patterns to re-focus consciousness. 'Focus 21' is described in the Institute literature:

> Focus 21 – like deep sleep, but with a significant difference. You are fully 'awake' and conscious, directing the action, as you explore more deeply your personal self and the far reaches of other realities.

The Institute's 'Guidelines' program uses hemi-sync to establish communication with the inner self, and includes 'direct training relating to the out-of-body state'. Yet more advanced programs are available.

Rapid eye movement or REM occurs during those periods of sleep when we dream. The eyes move rapidly from side to side. Recently developed is the DreamLight, a device that is worn as a mask over the eyes. Its purpose is to detect the onset of REM sleep, and then to flash red lights in the eyes. This flashing light appears within the dream as, for example, the flashing of room lights, a firework display or twinkling jewels. The dreamer has learnt to recognize these changes, and simultaneously to realise that he is dreaming.

There is also a standard method of triggering consciousness in the middle of a dream. If your dream record shows that a particular dream sequence is regularly repeated, then you imagine that sequence is happening and, at some point, you imagine examining your hands. Then, when that dream re-occurs, you become normally conscious at the point in the dream when you make the examination.

Alternatively you make up a dream which takes place in a familiar environment. You then imagine coming across some furniture, for example, that shouldn't be there, and imagine yourself reacting and realising that you are in a dream. By repeating this exercise, you will some night find yourself consciously assessing the reality of the furniture.

A variation of this requires that you visualize yourself back in the dream that you have just woken from. And as you re-run this dream, you tell yourself that the next time you dream, you will realise that you are dreaming. You repeatedly visualize yourself within the dream becoming conscious that you're dreaming until you fall asleep and, with luck, wake up dreaming.

Another method is to follow yourself as you fall asleep, into the dream state. This is done by focusing on the imagery that appears on the screen of your mind. If you keep doing this for long enough, you will become drawn into a fully-dimensional version of a particular mental image that has turned into a dream. It is possible to select an image with which to begin dreaming, by repeated visualization.

Or focus instead on your physical body, and feel it going into the 'trance' of sleep, while you remain alert. The body becomes numb, and the muscles seemingly paralysed. The 'inner' muscles of the dream body then respond as you will its separation from the physical body.

By asking yourself during the day, from time to time, whether or not you are dreaming, you develop a 'critical-reflective' attitude. By asking the question 'Am I Dreaming Or Not?' just as you fall asleep, it is possible to take this critical-reflective attitude with you into a dream where you will realise that you are dreaming.

You may have a 'false-awakening', when you think that you have woken up and are operating normally in the physical environment, until you notice some element of your surroundings that does not fit, and you realise that you are still dreaming.

Medical science is starting to take seriously the existence of the dream body; the reason being the accounts given by patients who 'return from the dead'. In the next chapter we take a look at the evidence of 'near-death' experiences.

Before attempting to leave your physical body, and to participate in your dreams, it is advisable to consult the books listed for this chapter in the bibliography. If you are experiencing a period of mental or psychological instability, or are simply not yet ready to leave your body, then the exercises contained in *The Nature of Personal Reality* by Jane Roberts are recommended.

CHAPTER SIX

Death

The evidence of Near-Death Experience, or NDE, is so powerful that it threatens the survival of Science's view of existence. And scientists are left having to ignore what they cannot account for. Most difficult for Science is the fact that observations are made of their surroundings by people who are clinically dead, and these observations which typically happen in hospitals can be checked.

NDEs are an ancient and widespread phenomenon. They are described in the Venerable Bede's *History of the English Church and People*, in Plato's *Republic*, and in the Egyptian and Tibetan *Books of the Dead*. More recently, Raymond A. Moody Jr, a psychiatrist with a Ph.D. in philosophy, has published the results of his research into NDE in his books *Life After Life* and *The Light Beyond*. He describes, for example, the case of a woman who left her body during surgery and floated into the hospital waiting-room, where she was surprised to see her daughter, whom she had not seen that day, wearing mismatched plaids. Once back in her physical body, she commented on her observation to the astonished maid who had dressed her daughter.

Another woman found herself out of her physical body in the hospital lobby where she heard her brother-in-law tell a friend that what with his sister-in-law's death being imminent, he would cancel a business trip so that he could be a pall-bearer at the funeral. She later reminded her brother-in-law of the conversation.

There is also the well-known case of a coronary patient named Maria in a Washington hospital. Maria had a cardiac arrest and later reported to the hospital social worker that she had found herself looking down from the ceiling at the doctors and nurses working on her physical body. She had then been distracted and had thought her way up the outside of the building to the third floor where she found herself 'eyeball to shoelace' with a tennis shoe which was on the window ledge in front of her. She noticed that the little toe of the shoe had been worn through and that the shoelace was under the heel. The social worker was intrigued by all this, and went to look for the shoe which she found. And there was the hole and the shoelace as Maria had described them.

Michael B. Sabom, professor of medicine at Emory University and staff physician at the Atlanta Veterans' Administration Medical Center, interviewed 32 cardiac patients who claimed to have left their bodies at the time of their heart attacks, and had therefore been witness to the attempts made to revive them. 26 gave correct, general descriptions of what had happened, and 6 gave very detailed and accurate accounts. Indeed the accuracy of one patient's account left Sabom stunned. He then interviewed 25 cardiac patients who had not had an out-of-body experience. It turned out that 20 of them made major mistakes when asked what they imagined had happened, 3 gave correct, general descriptions, and 2 did not have a clue.

Doctor Melvin Morse of Seattle, Washington, has interviewed every child survivor of cardiac arrest at his hospital over a ten year period. His interest in NDE was first aroused when he had resuscitated a seven year-old girl who had drowned. She had been comatose with a Glasgow Coma Score of three and was not expected to recover. But she did and later she described to Doctor Morse how she was watching him when he had been attempting to revive her. She had left her body, entered a tunnel and found herself in heaven where she met 'the Heavenly Father', who had asked if she wanted to stay or go back to be with her mother again. Over the ten year period of his interviews Doctor Morse became very used to hearing this sort of account of children passing through a tunnel and meeting kindly luminous beings.

There are even accounts of blind patients who, once out of their physical bodies, clearly perceive their hospital surroundings, later describing the colour and design of clothing and jewellery.

About one in ten people who go through a coronary care unit will have a NDE. This is the finding of the recent surveys conducted by Doctor Peter Fenwick, the Consultant Neuropsychiatrist at Maudsley Hospital, London, which identify those elements which are common to NDEs. The surveys show that about a third of NDEers go down a tunnel, about a third meet a 'Being of Light' and about a third come to some decision and are sent back. And it is usually the person who has the deeper NDE who experiences all three.

Whether the NDEer returns from the dead or not is determined by the 'life review" which he or she is prompted to experience by the Being of Light. The life review which is such a feature of modern-day NDEs is again to be found in Plato's *Republic*, the Tibetan and Egyptian *Books of the Dead*, and also the 2000 year-old writings of the Indian sage Patanjali. When referring to the life review, NDEers talk of a 'holographic', 'panoramic', 'wrap-around', three-dimensional replaying of their earthly lives. And every thought, emotion and sensation of their lives is re-experienced, but all within the instant that the life review takes. 'It's like climbing right inside a movie of your life', reports one NDEer. 'Every moment

14 The Ascent into the Empyrean *by Hieronymus Bosch
(Palazzo Ducale, Venice. Reproduced by permission)*

from every year of your life is played back in complete sensory detail. Total, total recall. And it all happens in an instant.'* Another remembers that 'the whole thing was really odd. I was there; I was actually seeing these flashbacks; I was actually walking through them, and it was so fast. Yet it was slow enough that I could take it all in.'† 'Not even your thoughts are lost . . . every thought was there,'†† adds another. And as well as the remembrance of our own thoughts, there is the re-experiencing of the pain of others caused by our thoughtlessness.

NDEers find themselves in a hologram-like body whose appearance is changed by their thoughts. They have the choice of taking a human form or of perhaps not bothering with form at all, experiencing themselves as a disembodied cloud of energy, as a 'cloud of colours and sounds', or as 'mist'.

When they describe their brief visits to the world beyond, NDEers talk of the light they perceive there. It is intensely bright. And they perceive within it the quality of love, intense universal love. It is light as it exists beyond our frequencies in the dream universe, and which the philosopher Plato described in his book *The Republic* as projecting our world:

> I want you to go on to picture the enlightenment or ignorance of our human condition somewhat as follows: Imagine an underground chamber, like a cave with an entrance open to the

---

* Joel L. Whitton and Joe Fisher, *Life Between Life* (New York: Doubleday, 1986), p. 39. Reproduced by permission.
† Raymond A. Moody, Jr, *Life After Life* (New York: Bantam Books, 1976), p. 68. Reproduced by permission.
†† Raymond A. Moody, Jr, *Reflections On Life After Life* (New York: Bantam Books, 1978), p. 35. Reproduced by permission.

15 Jacob's Ladder, *by William Blake*

daylight and running a long way underground. In this chamber there are men who have been prisoners there since they were children, their legs and necks being so fastened that they can only look straight ahead of them and cannot turn their heads. Behind them and above them a fire is burning, and between the fire and prisoners runs a road, in front of which a curtain-wall has been built, like the screen at puppet shows between the operators and their audience, above which they show their puppets. Imagine further that there are men carrying all sorts of gear along behind the curtain-wall, including figures of men and animals made of wood and stone and other materials, and that some of these men, as is natural, are talking, and some are not.

An odd picture, and an odd sort of prisoner, they are drawn from life. For tell me, do you think our prisoners could see anything of themselves or their fellows except shadows thrown by the fire on the wall of the cave opposite them? How could they see anything else if they were prevented from moving their heads all their lives? And would they see anything more of the objects carried along the road? Of course not. Then if they were able to talk to each other, would they not assume that the shadows they saw were real things? Inevitably. And if the wall of their prison opposite them reflected sound, don't you think that they would suppose, whenever one of the passers-by on the road spoke, that the voice belonged to the shadow passing before them? They would be bound to think so.

And so they would believe that the shadows of the objects we mentioned were in all respects real. Then think what would naturally happen to them if they were released from their bonds and cured of their delusions. Suppose one of them were let loose, and suddenly compelled to stand up and turn his head

16   *Plato's Cave*

61

and look and walk towards the fire; all these actions would be painful and he would be too dazzled to see properly the objects of which he used to see the shadows. So if he was told that what he used to see was mere illusion and that he was now nearer reality and seeing more correctly, because he was turned towards objects that were more real, and if on top of that he were compelled to say what each of the passing objects was when it was pointed out to him, don't you think he would be at a loss, and think that what he used to see was more real than the objects now being pointed out to him? And if he were made to look directly at the light of the fire, it would hurt his eyes and he would turn back and take refuge in the things he could see, which he would think really far clearer than the things being shown to him.

And if he were forcibly dragged up the steep and rocky ascent and not let go until he had been dragged out into the sunlight, the process would be a painful one, to which he would much object, and when he emerged into the light his eyes would be so overwhelmed by the brightness of it, that he wouldn't be able to see a single one of the things he was now told were real. Certainly not at first. He would need to grow accustomed to the light before he could see things in the world outside the cave. First he would find it easier to look at shadows, next at the reflections of men and other objects in water, and later at the objects themselves. After that he would find it easier to observe the heavenly bodies and the sky at night than by day, and to look at the light of the moon and the stars, rather than at the sun and its light. The thing he would be able to do at last would be to look directly at the sun, and observe its nature without using reflections or any other medium, but just as it is.

Later on he would come to the conclusion that it is the sun

that produced the changing seasons and years, and controls everything in the visible world, and is in a sense responsible for everything that he and his fellow-prisoners used to see. And when he thought of his first home and what passed for wisdom there, and of his fellow-prisoners, don't you think he would congratulate himself on his good fortune and be sorry for them? Very much so.

There was probably a certain amount of honour and glory to be won among the prisoners, and prizes for keen-sightedness for anyone who could remember the order of sequence among the passing shadows and so be best able to predict their future appearances. Will our released prisoner hanker after prizes? Won't he be more likely to feel, as Homer says, that he would far rather be 'a serf in the house of some landless man' or indeed anything else in the world, than live and think as they do? Yes, he would prefer anything to a life like theirs. Then what do you think would happen if he went back to sit in his old seat in the cave? Wouldn't his eyes be blinded by the darkness because he had come in suddenly out of the daylight? And if he had to discriminate between the shadows, in competition with the other prisoners, while he was still blinded and before his eyes got used to the darkness . . . a process that might take some time . . . wouldn't he be more likely to make a fool of himself? And they would say that his visit to the upper world had ruined his sight, and that the ascent was not even worth attempting. And if anyone tried to release them and lead them up, they would kill him if they could lay hands on him.

Now this simile must be connected, throughout, with what preceded it. The visible realm corresponds to the prison and the light of the fire in the prison to the power of the sun. And you won't go wrong if you connect the ascent into the upper world and the sight of the objects there with the upward progress of the mind into the intelligible realm . . . that's my guess which is what you are anxious to hear. The truth of the matter is, after all, known only to God. But in my opinion, for what it's worth, the final thing to be perceived only with difficulty, is the absolute form of Good; once seen, it is inferred to be responsible for everything right and good, producing in the visible realm light and the source of light, and being in the intelligible realm the controlling source of reality and intelligence. And anyone who is going to act rationally either in public or in private must perceive it.

You will perhaps also agree with me that it won't be surprising if those who get so far are unwilling to return to mundane affairs, and if their minds long to remain among higher things. That's what we should expect if our simile is to be trusted. Nor will you think it strange that anyone who descends from contemplation of the divine to the imperfection of human life should blunder and make a fool of himself, if, while still blinded and unaccustomed to the surrounding darkness, he's forcibly put on trial in the law-courts or elsewhere about the images of justice and their shadows, and made to dispute about the conception of justice held by men who have never seen absolute justice. But anyone with any sense will remember that the eyes may be unsighted in two ways, by a transition either from light to darkness or from darkness to light, and that the same distinction applies to the mind. So when he sees a mind confused and unable to see clearly he will not laugh without thinking, but will ask himself whether it has come from a clearer world and is confused by the unaccustomed darkness, or whether it is dazzled by the stronger light of the clearer world to which it has escaped from its previous ignorance.*

It is of interest that Plato, Pythagoras, Plutarch, Herodotus and Moses, who was half Egyptian, were all initiated into the ancient 'Mysteries of Osiris' by the Egyptian priesthood, and therefore had firsthand experience of the after-death environments of the dream universe.

That there is consciousness beyond waking consciousness was recognized by Professor William James, the American philosopher who died in 1910, in his lecture on the 'Varieties of Religious Experience':

The whole drift of my education goes to persuade me that the World of our present consciousness is only one out of many worlds that exist.

And:

Our normal waking consciousness, rational consciousness, is but one special type of consciousness, while all about it, parted from it by the flimsiest of screens, there are potential forms of consciousness entirely different.

He confirms this view in his *Afterdeath Journal of an American Philosopher* which has been psychically 'read' and written down by Jane Roberts. He refers to the light that he now perceives. It is 'more sparkling' than Earthly light, 'seemingly alive', and James describes in his journal becoming aware that he was being observed

---

* Translation by Desmond Lee, Plato, *The Republic* (Penguin Classics 1955, revised edition 1974) copyright H. D. P. Lee 1955, 1974. Reproduced by permission of Penguin Books Ltd.

by this unobtrusive, intelligent light. It seemed to be well-intentioned, and to invite contact. James realises that not only does he exist within the medium of this light but that he is himself formed out of it. He compares his constant study of the nature of light to a caveman looking up with wonder at the sun. And his after-death view of planet Earth he likens to the times in his youth when he would study the myriad life forms in a puddle. But because his senses are no longer tuned to our frequencies he perceives just the outline of physical events.

His experience after death includes the usual account of bewilderment which follows the realization that the slightest change of mind, or a vague desire, in some way generates entirely new surroundings. He discovers that buildings, for example, are formed and maintained by the joint belief of those who use them. And he has to remember to think his body into existence. This he likens to remembering to put on a hat before leaving home: 'of course it is not flesh and blood, though it seems to be when I want it to.'

Perhaps the main purpose of his journal is to let us know that from his new vantage point, his 'balcony seat' overlooking the world stage, it is apparent that we form, or rather our inner selves form for us, the events of our lives and the condition of our bodies. And in his chapter titled 'Biological Faith and Nature's Source', he states that any man or woman who succeeds in rediscovering biological faith will experience the complete regeneration of both body and mind.

William James and Frederic Myers struggled in their lifetimes to keep alive the idea that each man and woman has a soul (inner self). And in his journal James regrets that in life he concentrated too little on the evidence of out-of-body travel. Now with advances in medical technology, the accounts of patients who have experienced being out of their bodies are accumulating.

17   Professor William James (1842-1910)

If the evidence for out-of-body experience is examined by anyone who is not addicted to the materialist's viewpoint, it is apparent that science has made an error. Science is hardly the innocent bystander. The beliefs of science are again being used to justify the eugenic control of populations. The argument goes like this. We, as scientists, perceive no ultimate order in the Universe. So let us use genetics to impose our own order. We believe that in Nature only the fittest survive. And if what we do sometimes seems heartless and inhuman, it is only Natural.

What Charles Darwin, whose theory of evolution is so admired by the scientific community, failed to see was that his own vision was not sufficiently evolved to allow him the perception of the dream body of the prey animal as it is released at the point of death. Nor could he perceive the interaction of consciousness that takes place between predator and prey, or the inner communication and co-operation between all the species and the environment. All of this had been known in, for example, India for thousands of years, where it is easily understood that the mind, being free of physical 'camouflage', is the intelligent means with which to probe reality.

It is of interest that the existence of the dream body, usually called the astral body, has been widely accepted around the world. And under just about every cultural stone you find a belief in the possibility and practicality of out-of-body experience. Of 488 world societies included in a study by the anthropologist Erika Bourguignon – around 57% of all known societies – 437 believed in out-of-body experience. Michael Talbot points out that these experiences were known to the Ancient Egyptians, the North American Indians, the Chinese, the Greek philosophers, the medieval alchemists, the Oceanic peoples, the Hebrews . . .

CHAPTER SEVEN

Life

The French philosopher, René Descartes, wrote in the seventeenth century of the importance of the pineal gland in the human brain. He believed this gland to be the meeting-place of mind and matter. He had been reading the ancient Indian texts.

The pineal gland is oval-shaped, about the size of a pea, and lies between the two halves of the brain. Previously thought by science to be nothing more than an unimportant vestige of the species' evolution, it is today the fashionable subject of research.

It is at the pineal gland that the energy of our thoughts and mental images is transformed from its dream state into sparks of finer-than-atomic energy called prana. More precisely, this transformation relates to the chakra that underlies the pineal gland. This chakra operates as a unit with the corresponding chakra of the dream body, stepping down the energies of the dream state to the frequencies of the etheric body. These sparks or units of energy, which are the constituents of the etheric body, are vortices of electromagnetic energy that vibrate at frequencies just beyond the range of physical matter. The pineal gland responds to these frequencies. Put simply: our thoughts and mental images queue up at the pineal gland which then instructs the body's cells to reproduce them physically.

In Jane Roberts' books, Seth talks of the inner purpose of every nerve and fibre of the body, and of nerve impulses travelling invisibly along inner 'nerve pathways'. Descartes also refers to the 'animal spirits' that flow within the tubes of the nerves and the arteries. Animal spirits he defines as a subtle kind of air on the verge of ceasing to be material. They are of course describing Yoga's chakral system which distributes the energy of prana through channels or 'nadis' (see diagram).

The thoughts and images encoded within the energy units that are propelled through these channels are decoded by body chemicals which then communicate the decoded messages to the physical cells. For example, images of damaged skin being regenerated are directed to the skin's cells, triggering new activity in their genetic structure. However, this transformation of flesh only takes place if the units are of high enough intensity. A unit's intensity is derived from the intensity of emotional energy, of feeling behind the thought or image that it represents.

The energy units radiate out through the body into the air where they combine with other units of like polarity under laws of attraction and repulsion. The air itself is formed out of these units. A mental image, which has been transformed into energy units, therefore vibrates at the same rate as the surrounding air. This rate can be changed and an object deliberately materialized.

In his *Autobiography of a Yogi*, Paramahansa Yogananda gives an account of his time spent with an Indian named Vishuddhananda, who had studied Yoga's secrets under a Tibetan Master. Reputed to be centuries old, the Tibetan had taught him how to materialize objects. This had taken twelve years. Visited by the Calcutta intelligentsia, Vishuddhananda declared his purpose to be the demonstration of the power of God, saying that 'we too should manifest some of His infinite creative variety'. He would then

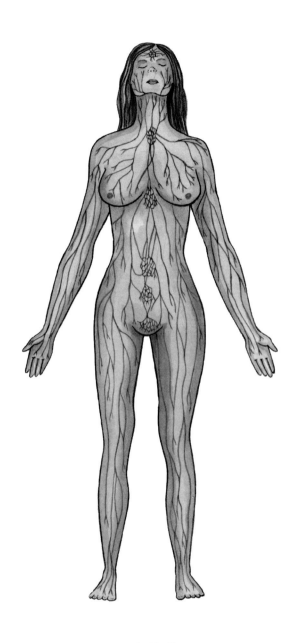

18 The Nadis

71

extract out of thin air whatever was requested.

Paramahansa Yogananda gives this explanation of how it is done. The body's sensory equipment reacts to the frequencies at which electrons and protons vibrate. This vibration in turn is regulated by the vibration of 'lifetrons' (energy units). Vishuddhananda attuned his consciousness to the frequencies of lifetrons, and rearranged their 'vibratory structure'.

In other words, he focused the inner vision of his third eye on the energy units and impressed their level of the frequency domain with a blueprint of the object. The rate of vibration was then stepped down to the physical frequencies of electrons and protons.

This process is reversible. For example, the human body may be dematerialized, becoming 'reabsorbed' in the etheric body. And there are accounts of yogis who have disappeared in mid-conversation.

The process of reabsorption can be taken stages further, with the etheric body being reabsorbed within the dream body, which in turn may be reabsorbed into other levels of the frequency domain. According to Seth, the physical body is being reabsorbed back through the frequency domain, and then re-projected out in space, all the time. The physical universe itself blinks on and off, but our level of consciousness recognises only the 'on-moments', and we therefore experience no gaps in time. Our situation is therefore comparable to the plight of actors in a movie who are quite unaware of the sequence of still frames that projects their reality. However, the yogi is able, from the waking state, to focus his consciousness through the third-eye vortex in, for example, the dream universe, making changes to the dream level of the frequency domain that are then projected out into daylight. He is able to visualize changes to his appearance and environment, and to control their materialization.

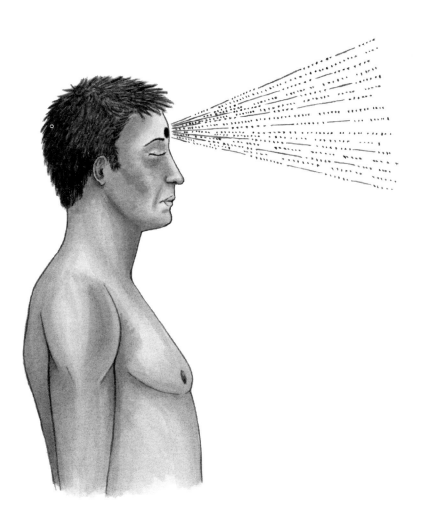

19   *The Third Eye directs the energy units*

Energy units are identified by inner sound, and their behaviour can be organized by the use of inner sound; by 'mantras'. Mantras are referred to in the Vedas, the sacred scriptures of India. The most potent and secret mantras are versions of the inner sounds heard by the great Indian sages in states of higher consciousness. Their sound vibration can dematerialize a slab of rock which can then be rematerialized at a new location. This is also true of the human body.

In ancient times, the misuse of mantras was excessive. Djwhal Khul comments that for the time being, the more effective mantras are being withheld from the generality of mankind.

CHAPTER EIGHT

Insight

There is a distinction to be made between reputable astrology and astrology that is simplified to the point of misinformation. Reputable astrologers are trained to know the types of energy that influence the planet at any time. These energies radiate from the seven stars of the Great Bear (Ursa Major), and are transmitted to our solar system via related constellations and their ruling planets.

The seven ray energies are:

1. The Ray of Power, Will or Purpose.
2. The Ray of Love – Wisdom.
3. The Ray of Active Creative Intelligence.
4. The Ray of Harmony, Beauty and Art.
5. The Ray of Concrete Science or Knowledge.
6. The Ray of Abstract Idealism and Devotion.
7. The Ray of Order or Ceremonial Magic.

The Fifth Ray is most potent at this time: its force being transmitted by the constellations of Aquarius, Sagittarius and Leo. Fifth Ray influence is apparent in the development of intellect. The Sixth Ray is now withdrawing its energy: its influence has been reducing since 1625 AD. However, the streaming in of Seventh Ray energy will bring about the fulfilment and expression of Sixth Ray ideals.

Djwhal Khul, the Tibetan Master who claims contact with Christ and the Buddha, has listed in his book *Esoteric Psychology* the effects that the incoming Seventh Ray will produce during the Aquarian Age.

The stimulation caused by this Ray will result in the much-predicted new world order. And in the dream world people will begin to link up with their souls (inner selves). The flow of energy through the chakral system is to be reorganized with energy being concentrated within the head. An increasing number of people will have achieved the opening of the Third Eye. And elementary magic will be practised as the species learns the new mental technology.

Both Djwhal Khul and Seth predict the return of Christ. It is to be in the next century that he will teach the methods whereby each person may contact his or her soul. Seth gives 2075 as the probable year by which he will have completed the work begun two thousand years ago. Seth is not prepared to give the date and place of his arrival beyond stating that two disciples are already in place, one near Calcutta and one in Indonesia. (Note: In 1971, when *Seth Speaks* was published, the African, 'a black man whose main work will be done in Indonesia', had not yet been born. If he is now living in Indonesia and there is a second disciple working in Calcutta, then it suggests that Christ's ministry will be based in that part of the world. The year 2075 is given in chapter twenty-one of *Seth Speaks*.)

In his *Treatise on Cosmic Fire*, Djwhal Khul predicts that the physical bodies of people who will be incarnating in two hundred years time are to be distinguished by their resilience and 'enormous physical magnetism', by their 'great strength and resistance' and by a 'delicacy and refinement of appearance as yet unknown'. And, not surprisingly, a prolongation of life through conscious control of the life-force (prana) will be experienced.

In his book *Esoteric Healing*, Djwhal Khul refers to the superior energies of faith that have the power to retard and negate disease. There is also the following reference to longevity:

> As regards the lengthening of the span of life during the past century of scientific attainment, I would point out that true techniques and the possibilities of organised soul action are always parodied and falsely demonstrated on the physical plane by the earlier scientific activities which are right in motive, but which are only a symbol, on the outer sphere of life, of coming and usually future soul action. The lifespan will eventually be shortened or lengthened at will by souls who consciously serve, and use the mechanism of the body as the instrument whereby the Plan is served.

It is now considered very modern when a member of the clergy comes out with the opinion that Christ's miracles never happened, that they are symbolic and not indicative of his ability to manipulate holographic reality. And as easily disregarded are the great ages described in the *Book of Genesis*. For example, we read that Adam lived for 930 years, Seth for 912 years, Enoch for 365 years, Methuselah for 969 years, Lamech for 777 years and Noah for 950 years. In *Genesis II* we read that Noah's son Shem lived for 600 years, and Abraham lived for 175 years.

On Wednesday the twentieth of February, 1980, Seth referred for the first time to seemingly impossible longevities:

> I mentioned that illness serves purposes – that it has a face saving quality in your society – so here I am speaking of the body's own ability. In that light the senses do not fade. Age alone never brought about any loss of physical agility, or of mental ability, or

of desire. Death must come to every living person, yet the time and the means are basically up to each individual.

This quote is to be found in Chapter 5 of *Dreams, 'Evolution' and Value Fulfillment, Volume One*. It is backed up by Seth's claim that there have been times on this planet when the consciousness of the human body itself has operated independently; times when the self-consciousness of the outer person had not yet been connected up to the physical body. And so, without our belief systems to contend with, there was greater agility and elegance expressed by a body that did not age as we do.

Finally, it is of interest that the Caduceus or staff of the Greek god Hermes which is sometimes used by the medical profession as a symbol was in ancient times the symbol for the third eye. With its two coiled serpents it represents the rising of the 'Kundalini' energy from the chakra at the base of the spine up into the head. And this is why you find that the traditional head-dress of the Egyptian pharaohs has a cobra's head in the position of the third eye at the centre of the forehead.

According to Djwhal Khul, in the future, society's healers will concern themselves with the stimulation and the balancing of the chakral currents. The chakra which is closest to and therefore controls the diseased area is first identified. The healer then directs his or her own energy into that chakra, creating a circulation of energy that permeates and heals the body by the drawing out of diseased atoms, and by their substitution. This is explained in *Esoteric Healing*.

The purpose of this book has been to loosen the stranglehold that the fundamentalist beliefs of Science exert on our minds: beliefs which seem sometimes to be more dear to scientists than their fellow men and women. Indeed, the behaviour of scientists

20   *The Greek god Hermes, with the Caduceus, symbol of the third eye*

21   Pharaoh with serpent symbol on the head-dress

80

often exhibits an emotional delinquency comparable to the intellectual shortcomings of people they have blithely categorized as less fit to live. The fact is that we all choose ahead of time, between lives, our mental and body types, and the challenges to be faced. A person, for example, who has developed lopsidedly, perhaps neglecting emotional development, but with an intellect of high calibre, will often choose in a subsequent life to develop as a more rounded human being.

An attempt is being made by establishment science to close out areas of speculation which counter the accepted wisdom that we are no more than soulless mechanisms, totally described by our physical genes. Scientists talk a lot about the Truth. The truth is that we are here to learn the undiscriminating quality of love, and to understand the creativity of the mind. This does not mean that we have to understand the physics of creativity any more than athletes need to have a medical appreciation of their musculature. But the inner self must be recognized as the provider of our experience by means unknown. We are given the faculty of imagination. We give ourselves beliefs. A belief in the power of imagination will soon change our lives.

EPILOGUE

Ancient Egypt, the Egypt of Seth and the sun queen Nefertiti, whose untimely disappearance so perplexes the mind of the dusting archaeologist and whose exhibited beauty was so admired by a dictator then inspired to genocide by the evil ideas of Darwin, was equally known for the conspicuous numbers of temple priests, whose activities, transdimensional and divine, were as unknown to the uneducated peasant of their time as they remain to the prejudiced academic of the present.

The purpose of the Egyptian priesthood was to map, through conscious exploration, those adjacent areas of inner reality and subconscious levels of the human psyche that have been referred to in this text. By imaginatively placing the pyramidal shape within the back of the human skull; by concentrating on the feeling in the back of the skull from which the pyramid forms, the priestess might then travel or ride upon a beam or ray of light into preselected and unearthly worlds, or visit those probable variants of our universe where similar selves wait to greet our evolving selves. The pyramid itself might seem to open from internal chamber into other world, turning inside upon its geometry that is representative of the gestalt of supernatural consciousness that originates those entities that are the Pantheon of archetypal beings from which our nature and Nature is derived and which we project outside ourselves by the naming and the classification of gods.

Through the continuum of consciousness, from outer to inner,

EPILOGUE

different points of exit and entrance were focused upon, so that the
attunement to the precise pattern of, for example, alpha brain-
waves by the psychic traveller is reproduced on arrival in the
otherworldly environment as the normal beta pattern in the brain
of the duplicate form of the projectionist. The pyramid's geometry
being superimposed upon the location of the main vortex, was em-
ployed by means of the psychic alignment of the priestess' mind, to
connect at the time of initiation the outer, embodied self with the
primal pulse of being from which the individual consciousness
continuously emerges. The pyramid and its vanishing point become internalised within the frame of the human body by the
realignment of the evolved personality with the vibration, the
'sheet of electricity' that characterises the plane of existence of the
involved inner self. Those divine qualities and attributes previously
projected beyond the self are assimilated within corporeal form by
transfiguration and the functioning of the previously latent power
of the third-eye vortex.

The projection of itself by the prime gestalt of consciousness as
the prototypical shape of the physically dimensioned pyramid is in
turn the human projection of a potent symbol which is by the
evolutionary process of enlightenment then internalised with the
reconnection by initiation to the inner psyche. Humanity, now
come of age, precipitates through the resulting third-eye vortex
those chosen forms and environments that are no longer forced
upon the passive apparatus of ignorant perception. By concentra-
tion upon the motivating underlying energies, enlightened
humanity forms new experience entirely, without time-lag and
delay, without the requirement for the intermediate medium of
scientific technology to which the dark forces of materialism
blindly have sworn their seemingly eternal allegiance.

Through the third-eye vortex reclaimed through the effort of evolution and the resurrection of the Goddess' energy in the minds and bodies of men, we reach through the stars, through the vanishing point to the light and timeless experience of divine consciousness. As human thoughts may be perceived as the constellations of deep space by astrologers of unseen worlds, so the brim of an unearthly hat may appear within this world as the plane upon which the Neanderthal ponders. As the chakras within our bodies through which like trap-doors we travel subconsciously, are the reflection of this planet's energetic co-ordination that reflects the chakral light of distant constellations, so the holograms of consciousness pulse through the grid layers of illusory maya, all according to universal law.

The violation of divine law that describes science's tampering with genetic systems against the natural course of evolution was through the black magician's informed use of mantra, effected prior to the biblical flood. Those intermediate forces operating from behind the scenes of Nature, performing the perpetual act of renewal and manifestation, being influenced by the more distant inner self's use of mantra and words of power according to natural law, were reached and a deliberate distortion of the evolutionary plan attempted. The two parallel evolutions of man and deva in separated universes, became confused as uninitiated man without contact or integration with the consciousness of the inner self on the Buddhic plane, sought direct influence over the creative aspect of the devas and the elemental lives and forces controlled by the materialising devas. That planetary chakra which links to the star Sirius and is the centre where the advanced initiates congregate in group consciousness beyond the physical veil, there to contemplate the progress of each species and the kingdoms of Nature, and relating in their supervisory rôle both to the distant consciousness of Sirius and to the planetary consciousness, then brought about the cleansing deluge.

Excerpts from the 'Seth Material'

Science has unfortunately bound up the minds of its own even most original thinkers, for they dare not stray from certain scientific principles. <u>All energy contains consciousness.</u> That one sentence is <u>basically</u> scientific heresy, and in many circles it is religious heresy as well. A recognition of that simple statement would indeed change your world.

– From a private session, July 12, 1979

Your genetic structure reacts to each thought that you have, to the state of your emotions, to your psychological climate. In your terms, it contains the physical history of the species in context with the probable future capabilities of the species. You choose your genetic structure so that it suits the challenges and capabilities of the species. You choose your genetic structure so that it suits the challenges and potentials that you have chosen.

– From session 910, April 23, 1980

To some important degree, cells possess curiosity, an impetus towards action, a sense of their own balance, and a sense of being individual while being, for example, a part of a tissue or an organ. The cell's identification biologically is highly connected with this [very] precise knowledge of its own shape, or sometimes shapes. Cells, then, know their own forms.

    – From session 913, May 5, 1980

No species <u>basically</u> biologically considers its own existence with other species except in a co-operative manner – that is, there is no basic competition between species. When you think that there is, you are reading nature wrong. Whatever man's conscious beliefs, on a biological level his genetic structure is intimately related to the structure of all other species.

    – From session 911, April 28, 1980

The animals are quite as familiar with faith, hope and charity as you are, and often exemplify it in their own frameworks of existence to a better extent. Any philosophy that promotes the idea that life is meaningless is biologically dangerous. It promotes feelings of despair that directly hamper genetic activity.

    – From session 912, April 30, 1980

Space travel, in your terms, will develop in a seemingly extravagant and startling fashion, only to be dumped as such when your scientists discover that space as you know it is a distortion, and that journeying from one so-called galaxy to another is done by divesting the physical body from camouflage. The vehicle of so-called space travel is mental and psychic mobility, in terms of psychic transformation of energy, enabling spontaneous and instantaneous mobility through the spacious present . . . As to the means, the very simplest and crudest but still to be adopted method will prove to be hypnosis, simply because at this point your personalities will not trust their own abilities but must rely upon suggestion from the outside.

    – From session 45, April 20, 1964

Space travel, when it occurs, will utilize expansion of self. Your idea of death is based upon your dependence upon the outer senses. You will learn that it is possible, <u>through no physical act,</u> to relinquish the physical body, expand the self, using atoms and molecules as stepping stones to a given destination, and reforming the physical body at the other end.

   – From session 55, May 20, 1964

Concentrate on the feeling in the back of your skull. The feeling itself is the important thing, for from it the pyramid shape will form. The pyramid may appear differently to each of you, because it is your own personal path into probable realities. It may appear as a path or ray of light or in some other form . . . Follow even further into the pyramid, which is a channel between your world and others that also exist.

   – From Seth/Jane Roberts ESP class

I do not imagine that this information will save the world. It will take more than myself <u>and twenty gods beside</u> to handle that problem . . . I do not pretend, either, to know definitely what is right and what is wrong for your universe. I may not know what is right for it, but I certainly know what is wrong. What is wrong is your limited perception. What is wrong are the arbitrary limitations which you have set upon reality; and these limitations, while set by you, nevertheless operate as if they were absolute.

   – From session 170, July 19, 1965

There will be a change in 100 years . . . when you will be able to see more . . . You will see through a growth of ability and consciousness . . . an enlargement . . . that has been growing for 500 years . . . the change began in the Middle Ages, existed briefly, died, then began again . . . It will involve an expansion

of consciousness, not physical knowledge . . . There is a give
and take between you and the stars on a physical basis, just as
there is also a connection between selves and what you call a
god.
– From session 203, October 28, 1965

The elements of the physical world that are unfortunate can be
changed in the twinkling of an eye through great expectations
. . . The true power is in the imagination which dares to specu-
late upon that which is not yet. The imagination, backed by
great expectations, can bring about almost any reality within the
range of probabilities.
– From session 891, December 26, 1979

Fear speaks for security. Fear causes to expect. The physical
symptoms of old age are the physical manifestations of fear in
the tissues. There is no reason why you, or any man, should not
be strong and vital until death.
– From session 145, April 12, 1965

But I also tell you that if you can change your belief in a split
second with enough strength and intensity, and reverse yourself
in mid-air so to speak, then the results could be instantaneous.
– From the Seth Audio Collection, Cassette One

NOTES: Excerpt from session 891 is reproduced from chapter 3,
Volume 1 of *Dreams, 'Evolution' and Value Fulfilment*. Excerpts
from sessions 910, 911, 912 and 913 are reproduced from chapter 7,
Volume 2 of *Dreams, 'Evolution' and Value Fulfilment*, published by
Amber-Allen Publishing. Excerpts from sessions 45 and 55 are re-
produced from *The Early Sessions: Book 2 of The Seth Material*.
Excerpt from session 145 is reproduced from *The Early Sessions:
Book 3 of The Seth Material;* session 170, from *The Early Sessions:*

APPENDIX ONE

Book 4 of The Seth Material; session 203, from *The Early Sessions: Book 5 of The Seth Material,* published by New Awareness Network. Excerpt from Seth/Jane Roberts ESP class is reproduced from *Adventures In Consciousness,* published by Moment Point Press. Cassette One from *Seth Audio Collection* is available from New Awareness Network. For further information, please see details in the Select Bibliography and Useful Addresses.

Seth Two speaks at ESP class

Our energy forms worlds. We help you maintain your lives, as you help maintain other existences of which you have no conscious knowledge. We watch you as you watch others, yet so vast is the distance that communication is difficult. We do not watch as human forms. You perceive us that way in distorted view. In your terms our forms would be geometrical. We do not understand the nature of the reality you are creating, even though the seeds were given to you by us. We respect it and revere it. Do not let the weak sounds of this voice confuse you. The strength behind it would form the world as you know it and sustain it for centuries.

The experiment continues. We are trying to appreciate the nature of your present existence, so those of you who are curious about the nature of nonphysical reality may then follow us, using this voice as a guideline into existence that . . . knows neither blood or tissue. Follow then beyond the knowledge of the flesh to those domains from which flesh is born. Feel the kernel of your consciousness rise beyond the knowledge of the seasons.

APPENDIX TWO

For you there may seem to be an unbearable loneliness, because you are so used to relating to the warm victory of flesh, and [here] there is no physical being with whom to relate. Yet beyond and within that isolation is a point of light that is consciousness. It pulses with the power behind all of the emotions you know; it feeds them and sends them sparkling and tumbling down into the reality that you recognize. This is the warmth that forms the pulse of physical existence, and yet is born from the very devotion of our isolation; that is born from creativity; that is beyond flesh and bone; that forms fingers without feeling fingers; that forms the seasons without knowing summer or winter; that creates the reality that you know, without itself experiencing it. From that devotion and creativity comes all that you know; and all of that has also been given to us. For the energy that we have is not ours alone, nor are we the source of it. It flows through us as it flows through you.

The experiment, then, continues as it always has. Only in your past you were not aware of it.

NOTE: Quotations are reproduced from *Adventures In Consciousness,* by Jane Roberts, published by Moment Point Press, 1999.

Nature of Consciousness: Wave and Particle

The distinguished philosopher and psychologist, William James, who died in 1910, refers in his book, *The Afterdeath Journal of an American Philosopher,* to his reluctance to pull rank on the reader by describing his new-found ability to follow a million thoughts simultaneously. Early man was, according to the ancient deity, Seth, in his book, *The Nature of the Psyche,* capable of following the rhythms of consciousness that we would define as being outside ourselves. He would allow his consciousness to merge with that of a stream that flows into a river and then into the ocean, at each stage of the journey experiencing an expansion to consciousness that had let go of the rigid boundaries that we accept in modern society. Not only could early man perceive immediately as being real the objects of his imagination, but he could become those objects, merging his mind with the awareness of the tree beneath whose shade he sat contemplating his life, at the same time identifying with that tree as being his 'tree-self'.

The development of the objectifying intellect came therefore at a price. No longer did man feel himself to be a part of this garden of Eden, this first paradise, over which his consciousness had spread out like a wave through the natural environment, but believed himself instead to be a prisoner, set apart from Nature, an outsider seemingly imprisoned within the skin of his body, quite unaware of the latent trigger of the female energy of kundalini built into his physical design, beneath the base of his spine, that was intended in the future to return him to the primordial knowledge of his oneness and natural harmony with the elements and creatures of the universe.

The adventure thus embarked upon by the species was high-risk, with the chance that we might lose our way, lose what we had gained in consciousness along the way, and fail to reconnect smoothly, when the intellect had been independently developed, with the originating consciousness of All That Is. The historical period of pretended ignorance by the surfacing personality of the outer ego would permit the development of a creativity, a new art of living, that was not practical before when we were too conscious of ourselves as thoughts, as mental processes existing within the cosmic mind of All That Is.

We were being given the chance to encounter reality from the perspective of the questioning observer, the scientist, outwardly separated from the divine embrace and omniscience of the cosmic mind that had responded to this human yearning to be set free, paradoxically, by the imprisonment of consciousness within the shape of the physical body, which was equipped, however, with a psychological escape route, a way back to the consciousness of the inner self. Humanity woke from the cosmic, paradisic dream, alone and at first frightened, for a long time forgetful of the purpose and challenge of this new type of solitary existence. The species had lost the capacity described in the two volumes of Seth's book, *Dreams, 'Evolution' and Value Fulfillment*, to alternate between the experience of consciousness as a wave and as a localized 'particle of identity', feeling as the consequence, abandoned to an unwanted fate, to this isolated state.

The inner self would retain the wave-like, ubiquitous and time-less consciousness that would oversee the progress through millennia of a species that perceived itself in isolation, as human particles apparently lost in space and time. A portion of the inner consciousness would operate the human body freeing up the outer personality for the pursuit of surface activities and the enjoyment of sensual pleasures. Cellular consciousness would continue to op-erate both as wave and particle, expressing the chromosomal information selected prior to each human incarnation. As a wave, as vibration, each cell, wherever located, would be conscious of the position and condition of every other cell on the planet's surface.

With blinding speed, the cells and the organs which they com-pose would calculate, between the moments of recognized reality, precognitively, the futures being imagined carelessly by this new kind of human who observed Nature from a single viewpoint, sci-entifically, categorising and planning with a logic trapped in the sequence of time. Each decision taken or not taken, each alternative course of action considered by the emotion and reasoning of the outer man, would generate a branching into parallel worlds where new human bodies would form instantly to reflect the different and multiple lives resulting from the intellect's freedom to choose, mo-ment by moment, from an infinity of latent events. At no time would any one individual perceive directly the environments being created by his or her companions who participate in apparently identical experience.

A rough equivalence of male and female lives would be experi-enced by each incarnating personality, to balance the psychic development towards integration, and for the same reason, lives within the different racial groups, inheriting the diversity of racial characteristics, would be successively led. The oppressor would become and know himself as the oppressed. The body's cells would dream within man's dreams, would each evolve into the organizing awareness of the various organs, into the consciousness of species, through the stages to human consciousness, and beyond.

All these historical progressions existing simultaneously within the consciousness of the cosmic mind, would proceed according to astrological timing, through the cyclical influence of cosmic rays on the exposed body, the chakras and the mind of man. From the ordered energy of the seven stellar rays supervising this planet's evolution, both the consciousness and forms, physical and pre-physical, of all life, animate and superficially inanimate, down to and beyond the atom, would emerge projected within the illusion of a holographic universe.

Excerpts from the mystical works of William Blake [1757-1827]

Both read the Bible day and night
But thou read'st black where I read white.
  The Everlasting Gospel

God appears, and God is Light,
To those poor souls who dwell in Night;
But does a Human Form display
To those who dwell in realms of Day.
  Book of Thel

For double the vision my eyes do see,
And a double vision is always with me.
With my inward eye 'tis an Old Man grey,
With my outward, a Thistle across my way.
  To Thomas Butts. 'With Happiness stretch'd across the Hills'

This life's five windows of the soul
Distorts the Heavens from pole to pole

And leads you to believe a lie
When you see with, not thro', the eye.
  The Everlasting Gospel

Man has no Body distinct from his Soul;
for that called Body is a portion of Soul
discerned by the five Senses, the chief
inlets of Soul in this age.
  The Marriage of Heaven and Hell, 'The Voice
  of the Devil'

Then I asked: 'Does a firm persuasion that a thing is so, make it
so?' He replied: All Poets believe that it does, and in ages of imagination this firm persuasion removed mountains, but many
are not capable of a firm persuasion of anything.
  The Marriage of Heaven and Hell, 'A Memorable Fancy:
  The Prophets Isaiah and Ezekiel . . .'

If the Sun and Moon should doubt
They'd immediately go out.
  Auguries of Innocence

He who shall teach the child to doubt
The rotting grave shall ne'er get out.
  Auguries of Innocence

Father, O father! what do we here
In this land of unbelief and fear?
The Land of Dreams is better far,
Above the light of the morning star.
  The Land of Dreams

NIGHT VISION

I see the Fourfold Man; the Humanity in deadly sleep,
And its fallen Emanation, the Spectre and its cruel Shadow.
I see the Past, Present, and Future existing all at once
Before me.
  Jerusalem

My Spectre around me night and day
Like a wild beast guards my way;
My Emanation far within
Weeps incessantly for my sin.
  My Spectre around me night and day

If the doors of perception were cleansed
 everything would appear to man as it is,
infinite.
  The Marriage of Heaven and Hell,
  'The ancient tradition . . . '

The Desire of Man being Infinite, the possession is Infinite, and
himself Infinite.
  There is no Natural Religion

Everything that lives,
Lives not alone, nor for itself.
  Book of Thel

A skylark wounded in the wing,
A cherubim does cease to sing.
  Auguries of Innocence

A Robin Redbreast in a cage
Puts all Heaven in a rage
  Auguries of Innocence

Farewell, green fields and happy groves,
Where flocks have took delight,
Where lambs have nibbled, silent moves
The feet of angels bright;
Unseen they pour blessing,
And joy without ceasing,
On each bud and blossom,
And each sleeping bosom."
    Songs of Innocence, 'The Lamb: Night'

Tiger! Tiger! burning bright
In the forests of the night,
What immortal hand or eye
Dare frame thy fearful symmetry?
    Songs of Experience, 'The Tiger'

SELECT BIBLIOGRAPHY

Chapter One   Kundalini

1. Yogananda, Paramahansa, *Autobiography of a Yogi*, Self-Realization Fellowship, CA, USA 1990

2. Krishna, Gopi, *The Purpose of Yoga*, UBS Publishers' Distributors, New Delhi 1993

3. Krishna, Gopi, *The Divine Possibilities in Man*, UBS Publishers' Distributors, New Delhi 1993

4. Kriyananda, Goswami, *The Spiritual Science of Kriya Yoga*, The Temple of Kriya Yoga, Chicago, USA 1992

5. Hewitt, James, *Teach Yourself Yoga*, Hodder Headline, London 1992

6. Mann, John and Lar Short, *The Body of Light*, Globe Press Books, New York 1990

7. Brunton, Dr. Paul, *The Secret Path*, Rider and Co, London 1994

8. Brunton, Dr. Paul, *The Quest of the Overself*, Samuel Weiser, York Beach, ME, USA 1970

9. Yogananda, Paramahansa, *The Divine Romance*, Self-Realization Fellowship, CA, USA 1992

10. Yogananda, Paramahansa, *Man's Eternal Quest*, Self-Realization Fellowship, CA, USA 1988

11. Brunton, Dr. Paul, *A Search in Secret India*, Samuel Weiser, York Beach, ME, USA 1994

12. Krishna, Gopi, *Living with Kundalini*, Shambhala Publications, CA, USA 1993

SELECT BIBLIOGRAPHY

13. Bailey, Alice A., *The Light of the Soul*, Lucis Publishing Company, New York 1997

14. Grof, Stanislav, *The Adventure of Self-Discovery*, State University of New York Press 1988

15. Grof, Christina and Stanislav, *The Stormy Search for the Self*, G.P. Putnam's Sons, New York 1992

16. Woodroffe, Sir John, *The Serpent Power*, Dover Publications, New York 1974

17. Bailey, Alice A., *A Treatise on Cosmic Fire*, Lucis Publishing Company, New York 1989

Chapter Two   Origins

1. Talbot, Michael, *The Holographic Universe*, Harper Perennial, New York 1992

2. Friedman, Norman, *Bridging Science and Spirit*, Living Lake Books, St. Louis, USA 1994

3. Friedman, Norman, *The Hidden Domain*, The Woodbridge Group, Eugene, OR, USA 1997

4. Grof, Stanislav, *Beyond the Brain*, State University of New York Press 1985

Chapter Three   Shamanism

1. Castaneda, Carlos, *The Teachings of Don Juan*, Simon and Schuster, Pocket Books, New York, NY 1974

2. Castaneda, Carlos, *A Separate Reality*, Penguin Books Ltd, Harmondsworth, Middlesex, England 1973

3. Castaneda, Carlos, *Journey to Ixtlan*, Penguin Books Ltd, Harmondsworth, Middlesex, England 1974

4. Castaneda, Carlos, *Tales of Power*, Simon and Schuster, New York, NY 1974

5. Castaneda, Carlos, *The Second Ring of Power*, Simon and Schuster, Touchstone Edition, New York, NY 1979

6. Castaneda, Carlos, *The Eagle's Gift,* Simon and Schuster, Pocket Books, New York, NY 1982

7. Castaneda, Carlos, *The Fire from Within,* Transworld Publishers, Black Swan Edition, London 1984

8. Castaneda, Carlos, *The Power of Silence,* Simon and Schuster, New York, NY 1987

9. Castaneda, Carlos, *The Art of Dreaming,* Harper Collins, New York, NY 1993

10. Castaneda, Carlos, *Magical Passes*, HarperCollins, New York 1998

11. Castaneda, Carlos, *The Active Side of Infinity*, Thorsons London 1999

12. Abelar, Taisha, *The Sorcerers' Crossing: A Woman's Journey*, Penguin Arkana, USA 1993

13. Donner, Florinda, *Being-in-Dreaming*, Harper San Francisco 1991

14. Sanchez, Victor, *The Teachings of Don Carlos,* Bear and Company Publishing, Santa Fe, New Mexico, USA 1995

15. Tunneshende, Merilyn, *Rainbow Serpent: The Magical Art of Sexual Energy*, Thorsons, London 1999

16. Mares, Theun, *Return of the Warriors: The Toltec Teachings*, Volume I, Lionheart Publishing, Cape Town 1995

17. Mares, Theun, *Cry of the Eagle: The Toltec Teachings*, Volume 2, Lionheart Publishing, Cape Town 1997. See appendix for video 'The Act of Perception'. Order direct from web site: www.toltec-foundation.org

18. Somé, Malidoma Patrice, *Of Water and the Spirit: Ritual, Magic, and Initiation in the Life of an African Shaman*, Penguin Arkana, USA 1995

19. Millman, Dan, *Way of the Peaceful Warrior*, H.J. Kramer, Inc., CA, USA 1984

20. Roads, Michael J., *Into a Timeless Realm*, H.J. Kramer, Inc., CA, USA 1995

21.   Wesselman, Hank, *Spiritwalker: Messages from the Future*, Bantam Books, New York 1996

Chapter Four   Paganism

1.   Roberts, Jane, *The Seth Material*, Buccaneer Books, US 1995
2.   Roberts, Jane, *Seth Speaks – The Eternal Validity of the Soul*, New World Library, CA, USA 1994
3.   Roberts, Jane, *The Nature of Personal Reality (A Seth Book)*, New World Library, CA, USA 1994
4.   Roberts, Jane, *The Early Sessions, Book 2 of The Seth Material*, New Awareness Network, Manhasset, New York 1997
5.   Peer, Marisa, *Forever Young*, Michael Joseph, London 1997
6   Guyonnaud, Dr J.P., *Self-Hypnosis step by step*, Souvenir Press, London 1996
7.   Kampf, Harold, *The Speed Technique to Alpha Meditation and Visualisation*, Quantum, UK 1995

Chapter Five   Dreams

1.   Stack, Rick, *Out-of-Body Adventures,* Contemporary Books, Chicago, USA 1988
2.   Roberts, Jane, *Seth, Dreams, and Projection of Consciousness*, New Awareness Network, Manhasset, New York 1998
3.   Buhlman, William, *Adventures Beyond The Body*, Harper San Francisco 1996
4.   Monroe, Robert A., *Journeys out of the Body*, Doubleday and Co, New York 1993
5.   Monroe, Robert A., *Far Journeys*, Doubleday and Co, New York 1993
6.   Monroe, Robert A., *Ultimate Journey*, Doubleday and Co, New York 1994
7.   Roberts, Jane, *The Unknown Reality (A Seth Book, Volumes 1 and 2)*, Amber-Allen Publishing, CA, USA 1996

8. Roberts, Jane, *Adventures in Consciousness*, Moment Point Press Inc., USA 1999

9. Roberts, Jane, *The Nature of the Psyche: Its Human Expression (A Seth Book)*, Amber-Allen Publishing, CA, USA 1996

10. Roberts, Jane, *The Individual and the Nature of Mass Events (A Seth Book)*, Amber-Allen Publishing, CA, USA 1995

11. Roberts, Jane, *The Magical Approach* (A Seth Book), Amber-Allen Publishing, CA, USA 1995

12. Roberts, Jane, *Dreams, 'Evolution', and Value Fulfillment (A Seth Book, Volumes 1 and 2)*, Amber-Allen Publishing, CA, USA 1997

13. Roberts, Jane, *The Way toward Health* (A Seth Book), Amber-Allen Publishing, CA, USA 1997

14. Watkins, Susan, *Conversations with Seth*, Moment Point Press Inc., USA 1999

15. Roberts, Jane, *The Early Sessions, Books 1 to 10 of The Seth Material*, New Awareness Network, Manhassett, New York 1997 onwards

Chapter Six   Death

1. Moody, Raymond A., Jr, *Life after Life*, Bantam Books, New York 1976

2. Moody, Raymond A., Jr, with Paul Perry, *The Light Beyond*, Bantam Books, New York 1989

3. Whitton, Joel L., and Joe Fisher, *Life Between Life*, Doubleday and Co, New York 1986

4. Roberts, Jane, *The Afterdeath Journal of an American Philosopher*, Prentice-Hall, NJ, USA 1978

5. Talbot, Michael, *The Holographic Universe*, Harper Perennial, New York 1992

6. Lee, Desmond, *Plato. The Republic*, Penguin Classics, London 1974

SELECT BIBLIOGRAPHY

Chapter Seven   LIfe

1. Roberts, Jane, *The Seth Material*, Buccaneer Books, US 1995
2. Bailey, Alice A., *A Treatise on Cosmic Fire*, Lucis Publishing Company, New York 1989
3. Bailey, Alice A., *A Treatise on White Magic*, Lucis Publishing Company, New York 1991

Chapter Eight   Insight

1. Bailey, Alice A., *Initiation, Human and Solar*, Lucis Publishing Company, New York 1977
2. Bailey, Alice A., *A Treatise on Cosmic Fire*, Lucis Publishing Company, New York 1989
3. Bailey, Alice A., *A Treatise on White Magic*, Lucis Publishing Company, New York 1991
4. Bailey, Alice A., *The Reappearance of the Christ*, Lucis Publishing Company, New York 1996
5. Bailey, Alice A., *The Externalisation of the Hierarchy*, Lucis Publishing Company, New York 1989
6. Bailey, Alice A., *A Treatise on the Seven Rays:*
    Volume I – Esoteric Psychology, Lucis Publishing Company, New York 1991
    Volume II – Esoteric Psychology, Lucis Publishing Company, New York 1988
    Volume III – Esoteric Astrology, Lucis Publishing Company, New York 1989
    Volume IV – Esoteric Healing, Lucis Publishing Company, New York 1988
    Volume V – The Rays and the Initiations, Lucis Publishing Company, New York 1988
    These are books of the Tibetan Master Djwhal Khul

USEFUL ADDRESSES

For information on Jane Roberts/Seth:
New Awareness Network
390 Plandome Road
Suite 200
Manhasset
New York 11030
U.S.A.
Tel: (516) 869-9108
http ://www.sethcenter.com

For information on the Kriya Yoga meditation technique:
Self-Realization Fellowship
3880 San Rafael Avenue
Los Angeles
California 90065
U.S.A.
Tel: (213) 225-2471
http://www.yogananda-srf.org

For information on the Monroe Institute:
The Monroe Institute
Route 1, Box 175
Faber
Virginia 22938
U.S.A.
Tel: (804) 361-1252
http://www.monroe-inst.com